BEYOND THE GREAT ESCAPE

Geoff Cornish: The one who got away

Helen Hayes

POSSUM PUBLISHING

First published in 2004 by Possum Publishing
PO Box 4252 Elanora, Queensland 4221

Designed and typeset in Bembo by Post Pre-press Group, Brisbane, Queensland
Cover photo by Geoff McLachlan, *Sunday Mail*
Author photo by S&S Gruzlewski
Photographs throughout from personal collection, G J Cornish
Printed in Australia by Cranbrook Colour

National Library of Australia
cataloguing-in-publication data:

Hayes, Helen.
Beyond the great escape: Geoff Cornish, the one who got away.

1st ed.
Bibliography
Includes index.

ISBN 0 9757015 0 9.

1. Cornish, Geoffrey, 1921– . 2. Physicians – Queensland – Biography.
3. Ex-prisoners of war – Queensland – Biography.
4. Prisoner-of-war escapes – Poland – Zagan – Personal narratives, Australian.
5. World War, 1939–1945 – Personal narratives, Australian. I. Title.

A 610.92

CONTENTS

	Preface	v
	Prologue	vii
1	Before the beginning	1
2	Monday's child	7
3	As the twig is bent	23
4	A beginning at last	34
5	Trained, tried and true	47
6	In the Bag	58
7	Apprentice kriegie	65
8	Stalag Luft III East	74
9	Highjinks and hellholes	87
10	One escape after another	99
11	Everybody out	109
12	The forced march	118
13	Witnessing holocaust	130
14	Go past go	135
15	Planning a future	144
16	Marriage and medicine	154
17	A real doctor	163
18	To the mainland	172
19	Paradise found	187
20	When I'm 64	192
21	'Heart over heels'	202
22	Maturity	207
23	What goes around	210
24	Due recognition	214
	Epilogue	221

For Geoff and Alison,
with love and gratitude

PREFACE

Geoff Cornish dreamed of being a doctor from the day that a doctor saved his baby brother's life. His determination took him through the RAF, a plane explosion, four years as a prisoner of war, escaping the Great Escape and the extraordinary experience of practising as a doctor before he had even been a medical student.

Marrying Myra, a girl with a lifelong illness led him towards another dream – keeping her alive against the realities of medical history and all odds. Ensuring that his wife created a record in cardiac rehabilitation led Geoff into a new, later life career in which he helped over 20 000 patients enjoy longer, quality lives and met his second wife, Alison. When 'almost 64' they married and took the Cornish Walking Programme to its zenith.

We meet Geoff through his tin-mining ancestors from Cornwall, his family, school, aircrew and prison camp mates, seeing indeed how 'the twig is bent'. Sometimes we can hear their very voices. We travel nostalgically through regional Australia in the twenties, the Great Depression and the fifties, refracting everyday life through the eyes of a truly extraordinary man. We meet some true characters from history during this journey through daily life. As a lifelong devotee of biography I hoped one day to write it. Meeting Geoff Cornish enabled that to happen.

Researching this story has taken me physically across the Australian continent, mentally to times and places which ceased to exist before I was born, and emotionally from tears to laughter and back again. Only a fraction of this rich tapestry of narrative has made its way into the book. Pictures maps, stories and memorabilia likewise. I only wish that I could produce a series so that not a drop would be wasted.

My sincere thanks are offered to:

Wilhelmina Beckers Mertens, Tara Brown, Tim Carroll, Alison, Geoff, Gordon, Meryl & Roy Cornish, Lisa Eady, Debbie and David Frith, Professor Greg Gass, Nick and Helen Gottschalk, Sheena & Stan Gruzlewski, Helen Heron, Michael & Guy Horsfall, Audrey & Brian Johnson, Professor Alex Kerr, Gary McKay MC, Dennis Newton, Adele Perry, Bruce Satchwell, Dr Eric Stephenson, Stephen Taylor, Sue Walker, Gwenith Williams.

Harrie Bahlin, Leah & Peter Bailey, Lorrene Brown, Sandra & Paul Burckhardt, Liz Chan, Bill Coppoolse, Lin Cox, Jim Ernest, Terry Evans, Glenys Foley, Maree Halstead, Robyn Haynes, Beth Humphries, Mare Kerwick, Maree Metcalfe, Judy Nolte, Possum, Dr Margaret Shapiro, Bet Skelsey, Rita Struthers, Rita Ward, Professor Gillian Whitlock, Marg Williams.

You have all helped in so many invaluable ways. It's *our* book, really.

Helen Hayes,
November 2004

PROLOGUE

We are sitting in the Gold Coast Arts Centre at a university graduation ceremony. The regular graduands are complete and a small elderly man is called. He looks like Chaucer in that robe. 'Not another old fart', whispers the young man next to me.

The man is Geoff Cornish and we hear a citation which relates his exploits as a bomber pilot, a prisoner of war, his bravery in bombing raids. We hear of his dozens of brushes with death, of being captured by the Nazis at only nineteen – the age of the young man. We hear about his exploits as a medical pioneer, the thousands of heart patients he has helped, his contribution to the community. Our university is awarding him an honour. He then talks about life, learning, how it all looks now at eighty years of age and how important it is to 'never give up.' This is his story.

Per Ardua ad Astra

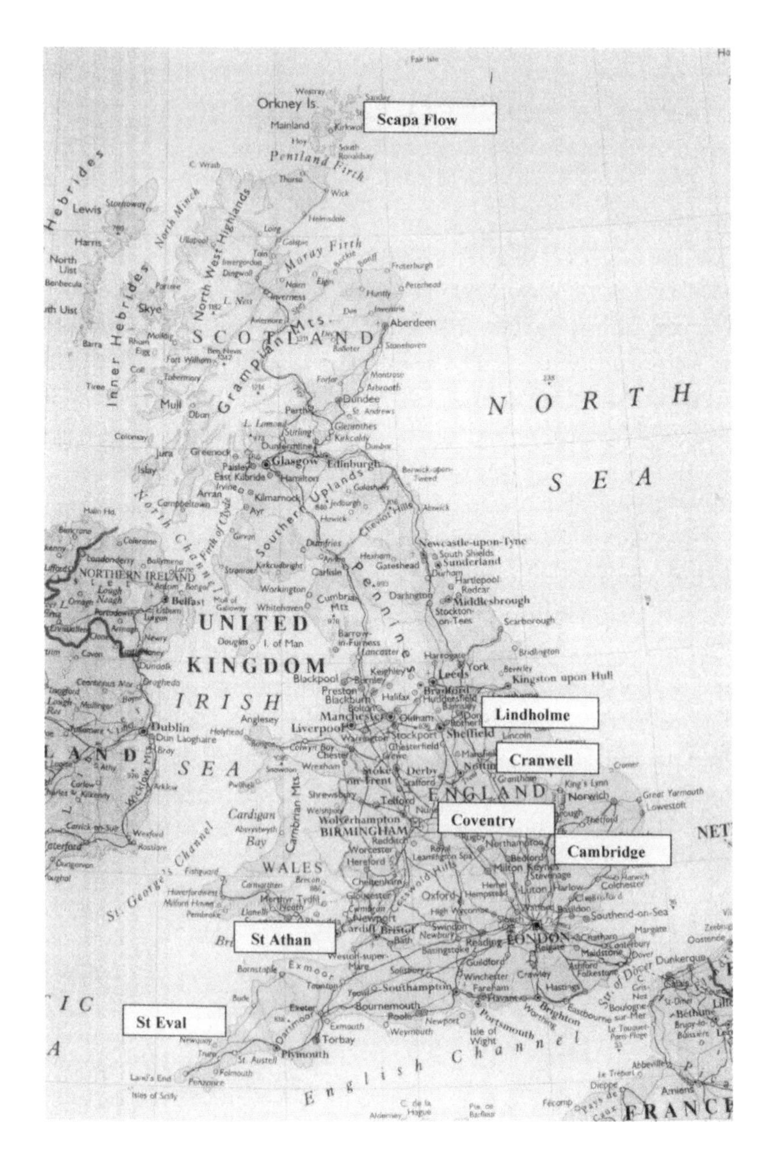

RAF BASES UK 1939

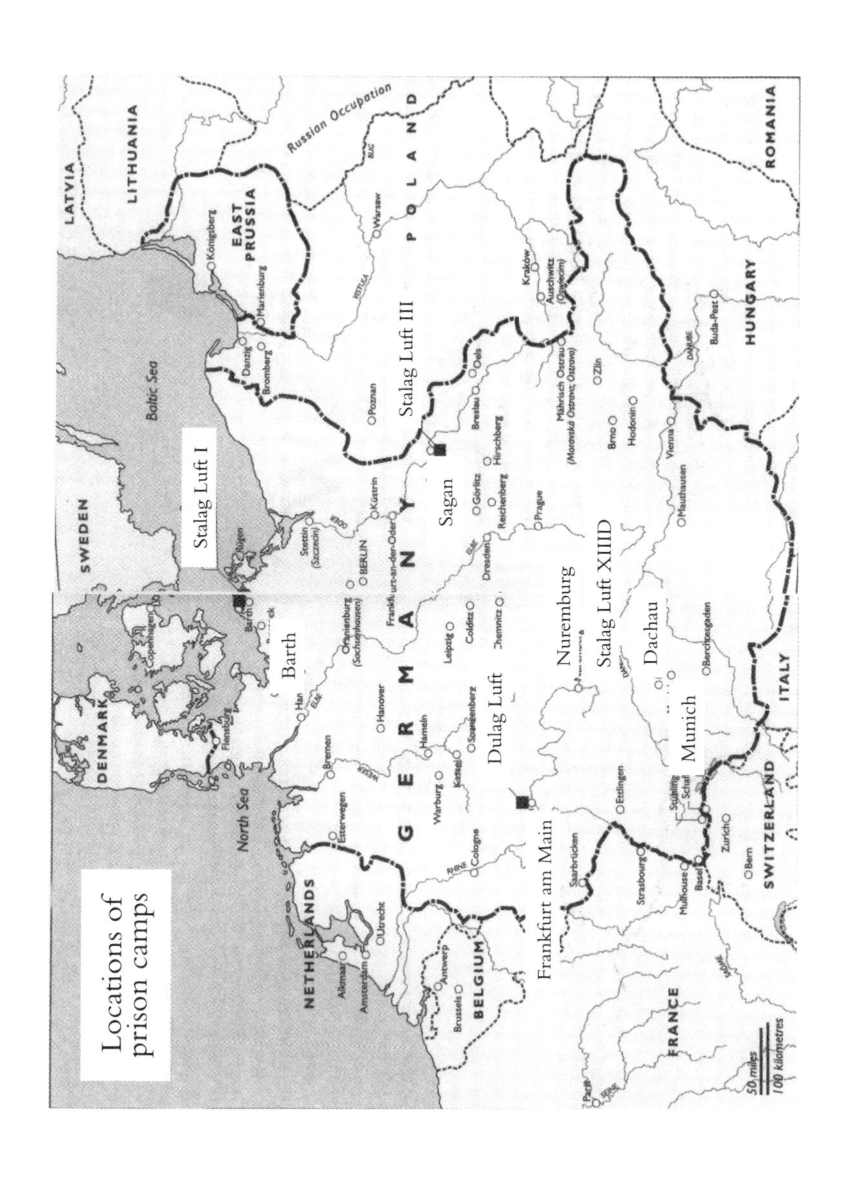

LOCATIONS OF PRISON CAMPS

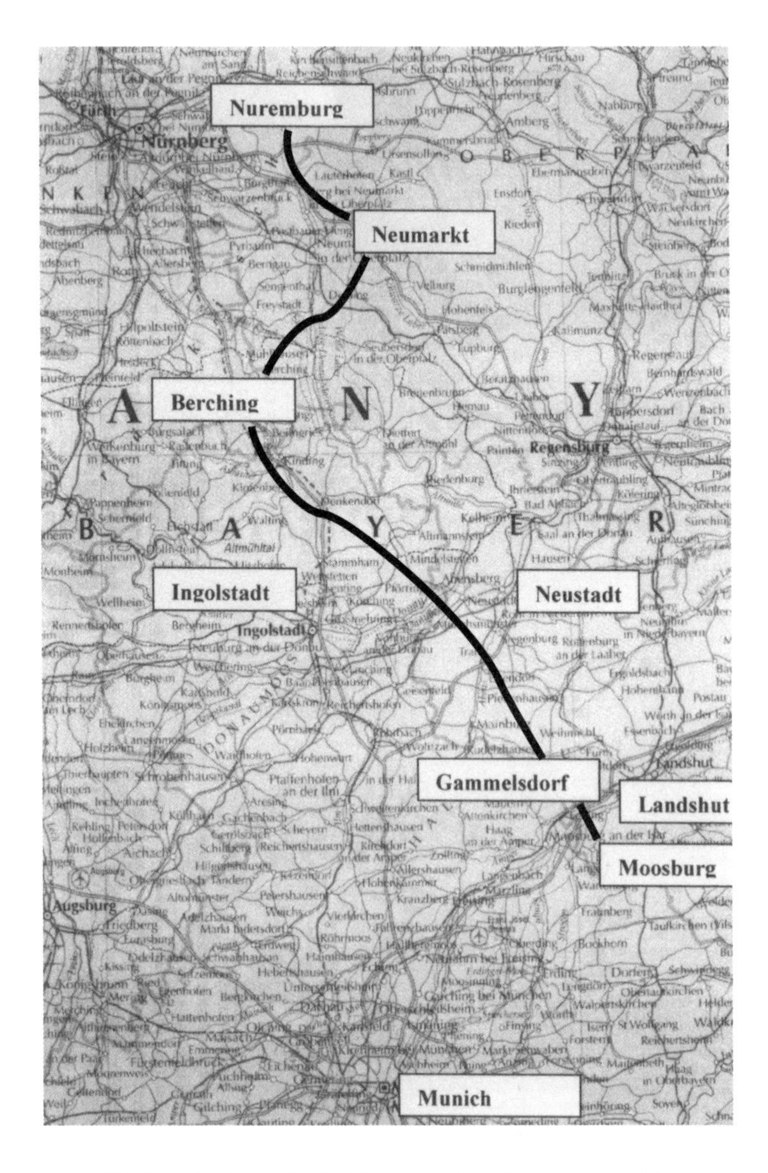

TERRAIN OF THE FORCED MARCH

1

Before the beginning

The Cornish family mined tin at Gwennap in Cornwall. When gold was discovered in Australia, Geoff's great-grandfather John, decided to leave.

John and Louisa Cornish sailed to Australia in 1866 aboard the clipper *Commodore Perry* with their three little boys. William, the eldest, was six years old when they reached Moreton Bay after three months at sea. Louisa and the boys could not have been more excited. John rowed the family inland up the Brisbane River to St Lucia where the University of Queensland stands today. They went ashore, selected a plot of land, felled some trees and started to build a house. They made furniture and began dairying.

The family's joy diminished in the face of the sultry climate, mosquitoes and midges and they agreed to sail south. It is not known whether John ever visited the Queensland goldfields but he did head for the Ballarat diggings in Victoria, where he found work. The 2004 Ballarat telephone directory boasts twelve families named Cornish.

William married in 1895 when he was thirty five and his wife Susan, twenty seven. Susan's father had witnessed the early Gold Rush and the 1854 Eureka Stockade. In 1897 William decided to follow the family custom of travelling to distant goldfields and left Susan behind with their two young sons. He headed to Kalgoorlie, Western Australia and worked on a water condensing plant there. The purified drinking water sold for two shillings and sixpence a gallon and he was able to save. Susan sailed to Bunbury with their two boys in 1898 and the family was reunited in Perth. They lived in a tent for a short while during which time William built the family's brick house at West Leederville. They had three more children of whom the only girl – Gwenith was born in 1912, seventeen years after the eldest. Gwenith would be a significant link between the families and the generations.

Fred Cornish, William's second son, began his education at West Leederville Primary School on 11 March 1901 and achieved fame for never missing a day in his whole six years there. In 2001, Fred's family presented the school with the set of medals, now framed, which their father had won every year for consistent attendance. Fred completed three years of secondary school before obtaining a job with the Western Australian Government Railways' Accounts Department as a clerk. More than fifty years later he retired from the position of Chief Accountant with the same department. In August 1915, aged nineteen, he signed up to go to war. He trained at Blackboy Hill Military Camp, fifteen miles east of Perth then went to Albany in the south, and embarked on 1 November 1915 to sail for Egypt to complete his military training.

He served as a signalman – Sapper – with the 4th Division Signal Company and with the British Expeditionary Forces at Marseilles from 8 June 1916. Fred was awarded a Military Medal on 21 October 1917, for 'Bravery in the Field' which was interpreted to the family as 'bringing back the rations'. He returned to Australia in June 1919. The family understood that Fred had witnessed things during the war which filled him with horror and made him a lifelong, fanatical teetotaller.

Fred always remained a member of the Returned Services League and attended memorial celebrations, unlike his older brother Joe who refused to do so. Joe had spent too many days in no man's land, recovering the bodies of his dead comrades. Joe said that commemoration 'only perpetuated war'.

Fred Cornish met his future wife Dot, in his earliest days at school, promising her that 'we will marry when we're old enough'. After the war he made good his promise.

Doris Amelia – 'Dot' Blackmore and her sister Cora, were born to 'a lovely mother' who died when Dot was eight years old. Her father remarried, to a stepmother with whom Dot was never happy. Dot's schooldays were lightened by Fred's presence. When in 1988 at 91 years of age, she was interviewed for the ninetieth anniversary of the school, she said:

> I started at West Leederville Primary School in 1905, aged seven. I only lived round the corner in Coldstream Street and we walked in those days. It took about six minutes.
>
> My mother was a lovely dressmaker and I remember we always had very pretty clothes. Somebody told me at one time that we were the best dressed children in West Leederville. I forget who it was but I never forgot them telling us because we thought we were just it and that was the year my mother died.
>
> We were thrilled to be there and my boyfriend was there. He lived round the corner and we always said we would get married when we were old enough and we did. I liked arithmetic and algebra and I finished up being a bookkeeper, anything to do with figures. But when we went for our world trip I was sorry I hadn't taken a bit more notice of geography.
>
> When the teacher wasn't looking I would nick down to the shop and buy chocolate and we'd have it when we got back inside school. The teacher seemed to be waiting at the door for me to come back. I did win the sympathy of the teacher, Mr. Ratter, a very nice man. I took a liking to him

> but I was always up to mischief. He told me to stop in the office one day which I did, and he said 'Dot why are you such a little tinker at school?' I said: 'well look, I've got a step-mother and this is the only chance I've got of having a bit of fun here and I have to get up to mischief'. I got away with murder after that. I enjoyed going to school.

Fred's family life is recalled by his sister Gwenith:

> . . . father was a bit of a jack-of-all-trades. Mum and Dad were foundation members of the West Leederville Methodist 'Endeavour' Church with the scroll of a psalm inside the door, and we all attended services there.

After Sunday school the family would go down to Monger's Lake where their father William conducted and played the cornet in the Brass Band in the rotunda which was built out over the water. His uniform was splendid, dark blue befrogged jacket and trousers with a red stripe down the outside. The children watched the little yachts on the lake while they listened to their father's music. The boys taught Gwenith how to row, to kick a football and to play cricket. When they went to the beach at Mosman's or Peppermint Grove by train they'd take a wicker hamper with the food inside and leather straps over the top to make it easier to carry. Their mother Susan, would mostly entertain people from the church and their 'hangers on' with high tea on Sundays. 'She would cook all day on Saturday preparing cold meats, trifle, fruit salad and other delights.' Susan was 'of a retiring nature' an excellent seamstress and a keen gardener. They had flowers and an extensive shade house down the side of the house. William grew vegetables in the backyard.

The family grew up in the era of the corner grocery store,

where you sat on a high stool while your goods were weighed and packed. The baker, butcher, and milkman came to the door, as did Gwen's favourite:

> The Chinaman in his greengrocer's cart. The quality of fruit and vegetables was excellent. The latter came fresh from his garden in Oxford Street, the fruit from the West Perth markets. An interesting sight to see him at work in his garden. A long tunic with full sleeves, loose knee-length trousers, bare feet and a conical straw hat on his head. A long pole was balanced across his shoulders, with buckets full of water at each end. He would jog trot between the rows and water the plants by leaning from side to side, thus gradually tipping the water out. When on his rounds he was dressed in spotlessly clean Western clothes.
>
> I would trace with my finger his name printed in fancy lettering on the side of the cart, TONG AH JONG, followed by Chinese characters. Quite often he would bring delicious Chinese confections for the Little Missy, which was one reason why I liked him so much.

When Joe and Fred left to serve in the First World War, Fred left Dot behind with his promise to return and marry. His sister Gwenith was four years old. She remembers watching her mother bake fruit cakes to send to the soldiers:

> In special tins with lids, she'd surround the cake with nuts in shells to hold them solid; the whole lot was then sewn into unbleached calico and the names were written on them in very thick black inky stuff. Although they took months to reach them, they always arrived in perfect condition. Dot often stayed with us at weekends when Fred was away.

Gwenith well remembers her brother Fred's return from the war. His papers show his arrival on the ship *Commonwealth* on 3 June 1919 after three years and three hundred and sixty days' service. The occasion was marked by Gwenith's first ride in a motor car:

> We went down to Fremantle to meet Fred coming back from the war. I think it was friends that took us, early morning we watched the sun rise, and we saw the troop ship come in laden, with all the soldiers along the edge. There was a rope to keep the crowd back. My mother pushed me under the rope so I was the first to greet the soldiers! Fred hardly knew me.

2

MONDAY'S CHILD

Fred and Dot were married on 18 September 1920, the year of an eclipse of the sun and the Prince of Wales's visit to Western Australia. The Prince's train was derailed in the south west but he was unhurt. School children were given a medal to commemorate the visit.

Their first child – Geoffrey James – was born nine months and two days later, on 20 June 1921, in a hospital half way down the Woolwich Street hill. The couple and their new baby lived in a rented house at Greenmount. Geoff was his mother's, the Blackmore family's first grandchild. Joe, the chemist, stayed away longer after the war and came back with a Welsh bride – Dolly, a beautiful soprano from Cardiff.

Fred soon built their war service home at 15 Joseph Street, West Leederville, just around the corner from his parents. Dot would live there almost until her death in 1992. At the time it was an outer suburb, some three miles from the centre of the City of Perth. The other four children were born at Joseph Street when home births had regained popularity. Keith arrived in 1923, Gordon in 1926, Audrey in 1930 and Roy in 1932. There were about thirty houses in the street and a dozen or so vacant blocks. When Geoff was five, he recalls that:

> Gordon had just come into our room. He was crying and crying. He was sick. I had to run and get the doctor. He was bleeding. I learnt later that it was his circumcision.

This is the first notion Geoff can remember of doctors, who 'come to your house and make you better'. His baby brother had been bleeding and after the doctor came he was well again. Geoff's speedy running was valued by the family both for fetching messages and for its use in emergencies. As the eldest child, Geoff appears to have had responsibility and authority in the family from a very young age.

The pretty tuck pointed cottage was everything that the young family could wish for. There were five steps up to the verandah. The parents' main bedroom and lounge room were located at the front of the house. A small bedroom opened off to the side of the dining room whilst the bathroom was immediately behind that. The wash house and the lavatory were outside, at the back. 'Mum's Domain', the kitchen, was the hub of activity. Many times over the years Dot declared that the threshold between her territory and Fred's was the back door: 'My department, right up to the very step!' As the family grew, the world descended into the Great Depression. Perth's population climbed to a quarter of a million people, of whom one third would at some point, be unemployed.

Fred loved the garden and grew an array of vegetables and flowers. He built a chook pen and eventually an aviary where he kept canaries. He and Geoff dug an eight foot long fish pond at the side of the house, when Geoff returned home after the war. The chicken enclosure was eventually replaced by a fernery. On visiting the house in the year 2002, the author found Fred's roses intact, thick stemmed and gnarled.

Fred's most famous vegetables were his peas. In the off season he would grow sweet peas which won him prizes year after year. On one famous occasion Dot decided that she would surprise the family with home made pea soup 'à la Fred'.

She picked the peas and made the soup. It wouldn't thicken. She picked and added more peas, and more. It still wouldn't thicken. Eventually in tears, she learned that pea soup was not made from fresh green peas.

Fred taught himself carpentry and over the years made many improvements to the house. He enclosed the back verandah to make a bedroom for the boys, which enabled their sister Audrey to have a room of her own. The children learned to mend their own shoes and to build billycarts. Geoff imitated his father by learning woodwork from a favourite teacher and walking once a week to Subiaco, to attend classes.

Fred made chests of drawers, meticulously dovetailed the joints, and painted every surface to perfection, which embellishment Dot considered to be excessive. 'If a thing's worth doing, it's worth doing well!' was the well worn phrase for which Fred was known. Dot was known for the converse – near enough's good enough'. They would argue, but never with any malice – over money, the children, and the contrast between Fred's perfectionism and Dot's pragmatism. For Fred and Dot there was no such thing as credit. There was usually no money to spare and if you couldn't pay for something you simply didn't have it. Life was frugal through the Depression and from the earliest time Geoff learned that you made your own fun and either made things yourself or saved until you could afford them. To this day the experience made him determined to improve things and improve himself, although he sheepishly admits to having lifelong trouble 'trying to learn to save.' Nevertheless, he was always able to spot an opportunity to earn.

One of Geoff's first attempts to make money was as

ringleader of a group who gathered wildflowers from Perth's Kings Park – blue enamel orchids, Kangaroo Paw, the prettiest of posies to sell to the neighbours. This enraged his father who did not consider expropriation of public property to be an acceptable way to improve one's financial station. 'He never let us develop a business plan!' Geoff still laments.

He practised calls heard at the footy – the shouting of the boys who sold peanuts and programmes, whom he envied and admired. 'Mum wouldn't let me do that – it was beneath their dignity. Dad was a very dignified man.'

Fred's adult grandchildren, Sue and Brian, describe him:

> Very Edwardian;
>
> A little fat man with skinny legs, he looked so funny in shorts;
>
> When he found out that the lollies were 'rum and butters' he threw them out of the [*car*] window, he wasn't going to touch rum!

The children grew up knowing that if you 'had a problem you went to Dad' and if you 'wanted something done you went to Mum'. Friends and neighbours alike knew that if something was amiss, 'Dot would fix it'. On the other hand if Dot wanted something done, Fred would comply 'only if he'd been asked, not told!' Father was well and truly in charge – 'Father knows best' was law.

In a way which so many people would not even know today, sharing was automatic within the family, the neighbourhood and the community. Unlike their progenitors, the family were not really churchgoers – Fred would attend 'once in a blue moon' and in later years Dot followed the Christian Science discipline for a while, but dropped it abruptly during the Second World War when her son Keith was killed in New

Guinea. The children however, did attend Methodist Sunday School and Geoff attended the YMCA and taught Sunday school for a number of years. There were still cleats in the floor of the Sunday school hall from earlier times. Geoff reactivated the equipment and held children's gym classes.

Fred and Dot 'adopted' for many years the daughter of a friend, after the girl's mother succumbed to a long term illness. They also contributed financially to the support of another family during the Depression, but the performance of these acts of kindness was discreet and done without fuss.

Family life was routine. Fred left for work each morning on his bicycle and in later years took the train. When Geoff was at Perth Boys' 'Tech' in the city, he would leave home on his bicycle alongside his father, 'but I didn't ride with him, I didn't want to be a sissy' he explains 'and I rode faster than him.'

Dot's household ran along lines typical of the times: Monday, washing; Tuesday, ironing; a day for everything: baking, shopping, mending, cleaning. Geoff elaborates:

> Monday, I'd chop the wood before school. Mum sorted clothes on the lawn in front of the washhouse. Whites went into the copper, then I'd chop the kindling - broken kero boxes, black-boy twigs, bits of jarrah. White clothes went into Sunlight soap – we cut up the old toilet soap, Dad only allowed us to chop up the very end. The copper stick was very white, and fuzzy at the end, rounded from the clothes and soap. You'd drag out the washing with the stick, into the rinse water, then shovel the clothes out into the draining rack and feed them into the wringer in the middle. The whites were rinsed in Reckitt's blue. 'Out of the blue comes the whitest wash.' That would take half the day. Then you'd wring the sheets and put them on the line, boil the coloureds and then do the 'non washables'. The things that couldn't go in the copper were washed by hand.

'Don't push the Dolly pegs too hard or they'll break!' The pegs were grey and shiny. By the time all of the first load was on the line the children could start taking the dry things off.

Shopping consisted of trips to the grocery store on the corner of Northwood Street near the school, to order provisions for delivery or choosing from delivery carts and vans which came to the house. In the twenties and thirties these still included the same Chinese greengrocer and the baker. A recent addition was the iceman – the 'Western Ice Cart'. Geoff recalls the enormous door on the butcher's coolroom and the huge timber chopping blocks standing in the sawdust on the floor. He liked to jump on the open back of the milkman's buggy to help ladle out the family's milk and ride with the baker in his van while trying to cadge a few tasty, warm bits of bread. Fred was so honest that on one occasion when a shopkeeper gave him threepence too much change, Fred took it back, although it entailed walking the mile or so back to Subiaco. Dot thought this ridiculous and the children thought it foolish. Geoff recalls: 'we were too worldly wise for that. To Dad, everything was black or white – you were either honest or a thief'.

None of the children ever forgot the time the minister came to dinner. They had been rigidly drilled that one never, ever slurped soup. The minister slurped his soup! They spluttered, coughed and nearly choked. Father kept a solemn, if very red, face.

On another occasion when the family had dinner guests, young Roy leaned over and scraped up some butter with his dinner knife. 'What do you think the butter knife's for?' his father roared. 'The visitors' Roy responded, having never before seen the single–purpose implement on the family dinner table.

Geoff cannot remember his first experience of the beach

but was told that he had followed his father into the waves when Keith was a baby. The toddler was fished out of the surf and severely admonished: he must never, ever go near the water without his father. They were regular beachgoers and Geoff doesn't remember actually learning to swim or surf. He and his friends would ride their bikes to the beach and before reaching their teens they were ocean fishing. Another source of income! As soon as Geoff was old enough he joined the surf club and would stay overnight at the clubhouse on Saturdays. He could catch the first waves before dawn on the beautifully clear and clean beach, be on patrol early and endlessly practise his resuscitation and rescue skills.

At five and a half years of age, Geoff started school at West Leederville Primary. In February 1927 it was two and a half decades after his father had commenced there and nearly ten years since Auntie Gwen had done so. Being a 'June baby' meant that Geoff was younger than average, and by learning quickly he skipped a year and moved into second grade after only a year. This probably left him comparatively immature, for which he would pay a price later in his education.

His friend Alex Kerr started on the same day and during the war was held in the same prison camp. In their eighties, the men are still friends albeit living on opposite sides of the Australian continent. Geoff, Alex and Geoff's brothers and sister share similar memories of the school, which differ only in detail and dates from those of Fred, Dot and Gwenith. Geoff's memories have been recorded by interview, Alex has compiled a memoir for his children and grandchildren, Gwenith has extensively documented her childhood and the times in which she grew up, and Dot's memories were audio recorded as part of the school's ninetieth anniversary celebrations in 1988.

The school was small when Dot and Fred were there but had grown markedly by the time their children attended. Alex remembers that in his first year 'plasticine figured large' and that he spent much of his time sitting on the classroom floor; Geoff, that there was lots of black sand and stumps to jump on.

They learned to write 'copperplate' and Geoff went home to practise at the kitchen table. Naturally a left hander, he was admonished by his father who insisted that he put the pencil in his right hand: 'Put it in the other hand, Son'. When he had that hand in plaster after the war and 'relearned' to write with his left, Geoff realised that if he first learnt a skill with his right hand, he could automatically perform it with his left. This experience later rendered him ambidextrous as a surgeon.

Geoff and Alex both recall more about the recreational than the academic side of their primary schooldays. Games in the school playground were mainly cricket and football with home made equipment such as kerosene cases for the wickets and sticks for goalposts. For recreation outside of the school grounds there was trolley racing, with the purpose-built trolleys being made from planks. They attached little wheels and sometimes the vehicles might even sport a braking system. The children would race these down the hill with someone watching at the bottom of the slope to prevent collisions. Even this construction experience would serve Geoff during his wartime days.

The trams which came down Woolwich Street were another source of amusement. Audrey relates the children's entertainment when these were 'derailed'. The contact pole would become dislodged from the overhead cable as the tram rounded the corner, and it would take an eternity for the driver, brandishing a long stick, to reinstate the pole on the cable so the tram could move on. The children's applause did not make it easier for the 'trammie'.

The teacher whom Geoff most clearly remembers is: 'Miss Crossley, the teacher in fifth grade, a stern old B, a real 'MISS', close to retiring, she taught my Mum and Dad. She was a good teacher, she didn't take any mucking around'. Dot had thought Miss Crossley was 'really nice'.

Geoff spent six years at West Leederville primary school. By the time his sister Audrey was in her final years there, war was raging in Europe. Her brother Geoff was flying with the RAF and became a prisoner of war before she completed primary school. The children played 'war' in the schoolyard, hiding in trenches and behind the trees.

Geoff spent much of his childhood enjoying the adventures that the suburbs offered. The limestone cliff faces, from which convicts had carved out the stone with which much of early Perth was built, were a favourite haunt. The boys would climb the cliffs, jumping from niche to niche, where the guards had stood to supervise the convict labourers. The young explorers followed the old railway line through the area, barefoot, and were chased away by the bandy-legged old ranger who looked after the site.

Walking the 'switchbacks' to the coast was an excursion. The switchbacks or the 'plank roads' consisted of two tracks made from planks, bolted end to end and sealed with a bitumen surface. These traversed the three steep hills between home and the coast and were so narrow that they had spaces along the way to allow vehicles to pass one another. Drivers would go really fast down the hills to build enough momentum to get to the top of the next. The switchbacks were used a great deal by young people going to the beach by bicycle or foot, and by horse riders. They could then follow the Old Perth Road around the coast, where the sand shone as white as the limestone cliffs from which it had eroded.

Behind Joseph Street was Connolly Street, of which much was vacant. The far side was owned exclusively by the Catholic Church, accommodating St Joseph's orphanage, the St John of

God Hospital and a convent for nuns who were nurses at the hospital. The convent ran a laundry. Between these properties and Lake Monger was an expanse of some 70–80 acres, a wonderful area for children. Lake Monger was full of fish; tadpoles hiding in amongst the reeds; and gilgies, the delicious western crustacean related to the east coast yabbie.

The children would go swimming in the lake after school and fish or catch gilgies. They would also paddle their canoes. 'Our part of the lake was very primitive, between Cambridge Street and the beach.'

At eleven or twelve Geoff acquired his first 'new' bike – an Excelsior, built by Joe Kidd the bootmaker who assembled bicycles as a sideline. This afforded Geoff much greater mobility, even though his prodigious running speeds had already allowed him to go almost anywhere he pleased.

The family had several matriarchs, although the favourite, 'Auntie Gwen' was probably more idolised than revered. Fred's young sister was only nine years older than Geoff. She adored children from when she was herself a small child so fell enthusiastically into the role of 'Auntie' to the Cornish brood. Gwenith tells us that her name is so spelt because of an error of the local registrar of births – the newsagent – whose faulty spelling Gwen's mother Susan, attributed to his being too fond of 'bending his arm' – drinking.

Gwen figured large in the children's lives. She remembers Geoff's birth and she looked after him and others as the subsequent children arrived. She taught Geoff many skills – especially cake decorating after he had already learned basic cookery from his mother. 'Auntie Gwen taught me to make a paper cornet as an icing sugar nozzle and then I did it for all the cakes. Dorothy Dixon from Number 21 Joseph Street asked me to do her wedding cake,' which was followed by orders for another four. He would exercise this mode of earning again as the student-father of a young baby, twenty years later. Gwen completed her primary education and graduated to Perth Modern Secondary School. She was vivacious and athletic and was a champion sportswoman there. She is appreciative to this day of having been allowed to stay at secondary school until final year. Her only disappointment was that her parents would not permit her to travel to Melbourne to train as a sports teacher.

Once a fortnight whilst going to school by train, Gwen would see Fred on the platform at Midland Station, accompanied by a porter with a large container of money on a hand trolley. It was the Railways' payroll. He was flanked by two policemen, and the brother and sister could not speak, only smile at one another. Gwen looked after Fred's boys and played with them at Waterman's Bay during a family holiday after Audrey had been born prematurely. The baby cried a lot and required her mother's full attention so the eighteen-year-old Gwen, who had recently become a teacher became a stand-in mother. She thrived on the opportunity to practise her skills. She took the boys, aged nine, seven and four, swimming and she and Fred helped each other with the cooking.

It is Gwenith's poetic recording of history that has given the whole clan a clear and colourful recollection of life gone by.

Family times were happy for the Joseph Street Cornishes. They made trips to the beach or the Lake and on really special occasions would go all the way to Fremantle, using Fred's Railway Gold Pass. The Gold Pass would also take the family on trips to the country to the various postings of 'Uncle Les'. Fred's brother, a station master, lived in various locations around the state. There was nothing the small boys liked more than going to visit him and being taken up to ride in the front of a locomotive, their tummies uptight. 'Why are they putting in more coal, Uncle Les?' the boys would ask. 'To get more steam, of course, to make us go faster.' Les, who was a good footballer, died young, of tetanus. Keith was a lot like his Uncle Les in appearance and manner, and ironically as it turned out, in having a relatively short life.

Eric was another uncle, Fred's brother, an accountant and a good musician. He played the pipe organ in Wesley Church and the family would sometimes go to listen. Despite Eric's skill, Les's prowess on violin and Gwenith's on piano and organ, Fred's children did not have a musical bone between them. Their grandfather William who had played the cornet here so long ago, then in the Kalgoorlie Municipal Band, returned after he retired to again play in the Monger's Lake rotunda on Sunday afternoons. Fred's children would now proudly attend to hear their grandpa playing. A sporting interest in common between the father and children was an occasional game on a friend's tennis court.

When Geoff was four he had his first girlfriend – Lois Pope, a brunette from Sunday School. By the time he was six he was still keen on Lois and wanted her to come to his birthday party. He went to put an invitation under her door and waited until there was nobody around, his heart pounding. She came to the party and gave him a present – a pencil case with a sliding lid and a place for his pencils, rubber and sharpener. She had even written a greeting underneath. He was thrilled and he treasured the gift for many years. Geoff was always cross that his birthday was in June, next to the shortest day, because it meant he had a shorter party than his friends – dusk came so much earlier then than it did at the summer kids' parties. 'I resented God for that!' He remembers the excitement of the kissing games.

The Cornish children all had their 'fair share of parties' and Dot cooked wonderful birthday cakes, fairy bread and other goodies. In time, Geoff helped with all these preparations for the younger children.

The boys made canoes to take out on Monger's Lake, from rusty iron, kerosene tins and bits of timber, sealed with bitumen which they scraped from the roads when they melted in the heat. The activity became legendary although Geoff admits that his own canoes 'always sank'. Every cohort and generation did this until one of Gordon's friends – Reggie Rowles – drowned there, after which they were ordered to stop the practice.

In those days everything was home cooked. Dot's staples included rice custard, roast lamb and beef stew, lamb through the mincer, shepherds' pie. Beef rissoles. Jelly and junket, which Geoff didn't like and trifle which he loved. Bread and butter custard, rice custard, fruit salad and banana custard were real treats. Patty cakes. She had trouble with sponges for a long time but once she got the hang of them, made them brilliantly.

Geoff learned to help with the cooking from an early age and to help with looking after the 'littlies'. 'I'd peel the potatoes and shell the peas.' He would watch as his mother rolled out a batch of scones on the marble slab and he would be allowed to sift the flour and shake it over the top. He would put them on the baking tray and watch through the hard glass door of the Metters gas oven as they cooked. He would make his younger brother Keith do the blacking of the stove and take the ashes to the compost. 'I used to bully him terribly. It was my right!' Geoff and Gordon were small, slight and curly haired, while Keith and Roy were tall, straight haired and of bigger build.

Cabbage and corned beef was a favourite: 'The best way to cook cabbage is with two teaspoons of water, a knob of butter, put the lid on really tight and keep shaking and tossing.' Bubble and squeak was scrumptious with onions and tomatoes.

Geoff's first memory of the Depression was 'when Mum said we couldn't have our weekly penny'. The children's 'weekly penny' was an institution – they each had jobs to do and if the tasks weren't done to their parents' satisfaction the penny would not be forthcoming. Except for during the straitened times of the Depression, the non appearance of pennies was rare.

Among Geoff's jobs in the household was maintenance of the Coolgardie safe, in which perishable foods were kept. The safe comprised a cupboard-like structure with wire mesh sides and a tray on top for holding water, and strips of hessian down the sides. The hessian dipped into the tray and siphoned the water, wick-like from the tray so that it seeped down the sides of the safe. The evaporation of the water in the breeze drew warmth from inside the safe, thus keeping the food inside fresh, or at best, actually causing it to become cooler. The Coolgardie, although an Australian Institution, was eventually replaced by the ice chest and much later by the refrigerator. Geoff's responsibility for the Coolgardie was to keep it clean, keep the contents tidy and to maintain the water level in the tray on the top. The other children all had jobs too, each progressing up the ladder of responsibility as they grew older. Audrey and Gordon would unwind their mother's skeins of wool to be rolled into balls for crochet. The boys had to put the chickens away in the evening, which could sometimes be a challenge when a stray chook or two would decide to be even more stupid than usual.

One night Geoff's brother Keith was in agony – doubled up with pain and screaming; their mother feared that he might be going to die. Fred decreed that Geoff must go on his bike to the hospital, as fast as he possibly could, to fetch the doctor. Geoff's heart was racing; he was sweating and panting when he reached the hospital. The doctor came, with his big black bag, examined the boy and sent him straight to hospital with a burst appendix. It was serious and Keith was in hospital for a couple of weeks. The image of 'doctor' was by now consolidating in Geoff's unconscious mind.

At the end of 1932 Geoff left West Leederville Primary School and commenced studies at Perth Secondary Boys' Technical School in Roe Street, between James and Francis Streets, past the horseshoe bridge. Roe Street was the home of Perth's brothels and nearby Beaufort Street was where his father worked at the Railways Department.

Geoff's final primary school report noted: 'a definite scientific bent, which should be encouraged'. In secondary school Geoff took the maximum possible number of science subjects, including geology, his interest in the latter having been generated by his friends' fathers being miners and prospectors. That alerted the boys to the potential riches to be found in the exploration industries. Geoff's years at full time secondary school were as academically unexciting as his primary years had been, with extracurricular and sporting activities still offering far more interest and excitement.

One innovation at the school while Tommy Chandler was the headmaster, was the teacher 'travelling' upwards with their class: 'Pud' Smallwood moved up with the group for the three years that Geoff was there. During this time 'Pud' exhorted Geoff to give up Australian Rules football and adopt rugby. He feared that the small and slight young man might be crushed to pieces in that rough game, and moreover could use his stature and skills to greater advantage. 'He said I'd be clobbered playing Aussie rules, and that I'd do well at rugby. I was a fast runner. I always ran for Mum's messages and quickly became a good rugby union tackler.' The teacher taught Geoff the new game and watched him become a competent scrum half.

Fred Cornish only talked to his sons about the war when he considered they were 'grown up enough' and even then at a minimum. He always participated in the Anzac Day marches. The children polished his medals, accompanied him to the dawn service and watched the march. They attended the 'Sons of Soldiers League' which Fred considered to be important 'in case the RSL should ever die out'. He also ensured that his children 'never did anything military'.

Geoff loved nature studies and his science subjects at school. When he had read a book about designing your own experiments, the master allowed him to demonstrate one of the classics, to the class. He gravely placed a lighted candle in a bowl with a glass cylinder over the candle. The burning of the candle would use up all the oxygen inside the cylinder and when the oxygen was all gone the water would rise up in the cylinder to replace it.

An eagerly anticipated annual event was Guy Fawkes' or 'bonfire night'. A commemoration inherited from 'the old country' it celebrated a failed plot to blow up the British Houses of Parliament in 1605. Children across Australia constructed and ignited massive bonfires, accompanied by fireworks and by the burning of a 'Guy' signifying the demise and beheading of the original plotter. Our young heroes would construct their 'Guy' and before the fire, parade him around the district to raise funds for the purchase of fireworks. Alex Kerr remembers sitting with his 'Guy' at the entrance to the local station, 'soliciting' pennies from the evening commuters. The eventual fire would be accompanied by a blaze of 'crackers' – penny bungers, sky rockets, Catherine wheels and jumping jacks.

Geoff remembers the Empire theatre being built, in Cambridge St between the school and the railway station. Saturday afternoon Westerns were accompanied by shouting, stamping of feet and the gobbling down of bagsful of broken biscuits purchased from the Northwood Street shop near the school.

3

AS THE TWIG IS BENT

When Geoff turned fourteen it was time to leave school, find a job and help to support the family, as was the norm. Fred asked: 'What do you want to do, Son?' 'I want to be a doctor.' Geoff later observed: 'He must have thought I was mad or that he had a son who was terribly stubborn.'

So Geoff left school at the end of 1935 and commenced a job as office boy with the firm Reath and Lapsley, Public Analysts in St George's Terrace in February 1936. He was paid seven shillings and sixpence a week (75 cents) and continued his secondary education at night school. Reath and Lapsley analysed geological samples brought in by prospectors, an aspect of the work which excited Geoff immensely. Sometimes he and his friends would travel to the outback on a weekend, using Bill Pepper's father's Pontiac, and find enough gold to pay for petrol, clean and garage the car and each have a tidy profit left over.

In early 1937, as Reath and Lapsley went into decline, the University of Western Australia sought a chemistry Cadet. Not only did our hero spot the advertisement on the night school notice board, but he removed the card so that no one else could apply. He obtained the position in February 1937 and worked at the University for three years. Geoff explains:

> Cadet was a nice name for cleaner. I had a long white coat which I had to pay for myself out of my wages, which were

> again seven and six a week. I had to sweep all the floors, dust all the offices, do all the bottles, clear the bins and put out the students' frequent ether fires.

The position allowed the occupant ten hours study leave per week to go to senior Technical College in Perth, during day-light working hours. Geoff would cycle from the University into Perth at eleven o'clock for chemistry class, three miles home at one o'clock for lunch, back to work from two until five in the afternoon, then home again for the evening meal. He would then cycle the three miles back into senior tech for night school on Monday, Tuesday, Thursday and Friday evenings, from seven to ten pm.

In the morning he would be back on his bike at five o'clock to go out to the surf with his mates, riding single file along the planks so as not to get their tyres stuck in the com-pacted sand between them. A very energetic, but to Geoff's mind, a balanced life.

Another joy was going surfing after night school. Again, the Pontiac enabled the boys to get quickly to the beach after class, have a surf, dry their hair in the exhaust of the vehicle and be home before their parents even suspected that they'd done a detour.

Somewhere in this period Geoff recalls that he had a memorable holiday at the country property of his Auntie Gwen and Uncle Syd. Gwenith had been appointed teacher in the country, met her future husband there, and finally become engaged and married.

In her early years in the country Gwen had played tennis on Sunday, for which her strict Methodist upbringing had led her to expect to be 'struck down'. She played cards with the country locals and had a holiday at Cottesloe beach with Syd, her 'intended' who proposed to her while they were there.

When Gwenith and Sydney were married, Geoff performed a recitation at their wedding. At some point thereafter Geoff says that he went on holiday to their farm. The story is vague, because although Geoff declares his memory of the incident 'perfect', 'Auntie Gwen' to this day has no recollection of him ever visiting the farm. Geoff's story goes:

> They drove me back; they were newly married. They had about two thousand acres. Syd had gone off to the paddocks. I noticed a rabbit run by and disappear into a pile of wood. 'Dinner.' I thought, 'I must get that rabbit!' I started to move the wood, log by log, to get to the rabbit, really quite a big job. I'd moved about one tenth of the timber out onto the path, when Syd returned with the machinery pulled by his eight Clydesdales which were all addressed by name. The logs I'd moved were right on his path and he couldn't possibly get the horses past them. I don't really remember what happened exactly except that Syd had to get the horses past and had to work awfully hard to get the wood out of the way. We didn't have rabbit stew that night, or any other. I adored Syd.

One possible explanation for the discrepancy in this story might be that Uncle Syd had been kind enough to not tell his new wife of her nephew's escapade.

Geoff's early working years were marked by evenings and weekends at the YMCA where he met his hero and mentor, Ivor Hanger. Mr Hanger had an immediate impact upon Geoff: 'He was a lovely man, a Queenslander, newly appointed. I found that with Ivor I had a great mentor and friend'. On Wednesday evenings Geoff attended the 'Y' for gymnasium and other activities, including swimming in the only indoor pool in Perth.

The YMCA was a strong Christian influence at the time,

especially for Geoff. The 'Y' conducted different 'clubs' on the different days of the week. The club which Geoff attended was called the 'Four Square Club' based upon a biblical quotation:

> *Jesus increased in wisdom and stature and in favour with God and man.*
>
> (Luke, II, 52)

Ivor exhorted the young men to base their lives on the quotation. He asked the young men to increase in wisdom, reflecting mental development, stature which represented physical development, in favour with God, which was philosophical and theological development, and with Man – their social obligations to family and community. The aim was for the individual to expand and develop his life evenly along those four axes.

One Wednesday Mr Hanger announced: 'Boys, I've drawn up a chart on each of you'. The chart consisted of two straight lines intersecting at right angles, marked one to ten from the centre. Geoff's chart was chosen first because he was the current leader. 'Now boys, pick Geoff's chart to pieces!'

> Mental – he'd given me quite a high score because of my night school activities; Physical – fairly high because of the YMCA activities and the swimming. I went to Sunday School and to the Methodist Church, and I was quite an honest Christian. I got two for social activities.
>
> So the boys said: 'What's wrong with you?'
>
> They were then the jury to decide my fate: 'Have you got a girlfriend?'
>
> 'No.' 'Why not?'
>
> 'I just don't have time for one right now – I don't have the money for one thing.'
>
> 'They said "right, we'll fix that. We've got to sort that side

of your life out to get a high score there. We're going to the YWCA dance on Saturday night".'

'I'm not, I can't dance.' 'They said "neither can the girls, and the first hour is a dancing class".'

So there was no dodging it. Geoff attended and found that the girls were quite human and trod on the boys' toes as often as they did theirs. They had lots of fun and laughs. He continued to attend and soon had girlfriends.

The next time Geoff was assessed, his score improved and he was named 'clubman of the month' for having the closest score to a perfect square.

Seventy years later, Geoff muses:

> That little saying, that attitude, has helped me in every situation I've ever been in. It's helped me tremendously as a doctor, because I model my questioning on those four lines. What's your hobby? How do you keep yourself mentally alive? Physical activities? Serious thinking, family, and so on. I score them simply, then look with them at where they need to work to get their life into balance. It works in every situation. It also helped me immensely when I was a prisoner of war.
>
> There, unfortunately, we lost two or three guys who absolutely flipped. But there were a hell of a lot we saved because we were able to direct their activities without them realising that they were being directed. There were no ranks of course, you were shoulder to shoulder with the next bloke. Many of us, including the senior Germans were aware of the importance of damage control.

Most weekends were spent at the City Beach Surf Life Saving Club and Geoff applied himself assiduously to learning resuscitation skills. The instructors at the surf club, men in their early twenties, gave their time to teach the younger ones lifesaving. They were greatly admired, excellent surfers, brilliant swimmers and usually patient teachers. Geoff learned the Schäffer method of resuscitation which he says 'entailed kneeling beside the person with thumbs apart, exerting three seconds of downward pressure, two seconds of no pressure then another three seconds of downward pressure'. Meticulous timing was required, which suited Geoff down to the ground. He was always assigned to resuscitation in the surf team. In competition, points would be lost for every second's inaccuracy. Geoff was the first member of his family to join the City of Perth Surf Life Saving Club, but his three brothers and sister followed over the years. They all took up lifesaving duties, running up and down the sand and into the surf, keeping themselves physically fit. Everyone had to be tanned to perfection – absolutely black – before the summer even started. All were fair skinned and blue eyed and knew nothing at the time about the risk of melanoma. 'But I do now!' Geoff says sadly in the next millennium.

In Geoff's working environment, he found another opportunity to use his timing skills. The chemistry school had a beautiful, architect designed, photographic laboratory, an enormous darkroom, which was seldom used. He gained permission to use it and he had free use of chemicals and equipment. By doing photographic developing and printing for friends and members of the University, he doubled his wage! He learned to time the period that the film stayed in the developing fluid, by closing his eyes and counting. He checked the clock every minute or two to sharpen his accuracy. Although he had learned at a young age that one could never know when a skill or piece of knowledge might come in handy, he could not have dreamed what this photographic knowledge would do for him later.

While Geoff was cleaning the laboratory or setting out the chemicals for demonstrations, a professor called Noel Stanley Bayliss would sometimes come in and sit astride the bench. 'Any problems?' he would ask. He'd talk with Geoff, give him his time and interest. When Geoff returned to Perth after the war, Bayliss was one of the first people he sought out.

Although Geoff continued to attend all of his night school classes his attention to studying outside of class was not what it might have been. He failed his final year, gaining an honour for English but not another single pass. Geoff was surprised and his father was furious. The following year when Geoff was compelled to repeat the subjects, he thought it would be easy. Fred decided to join – or rather shadow – his son. He obtained the full lecture syllabus, examined it, and made a practice of waiting for his son to come home. At midnight, there would be Father, sitting expectantly at the dining room table:

> He would ask me what I'd learnt that night. I bluffed, but I could tell that he knew. He thought that because I was repeating, if I paid attention, I could easily teach him. God I thought Dad was a dumb bugger!

Fred went through the text books and grilled his son. Eventually, Geoff realised that if he paid attention he could learn easily. He also eventually understood that his father was genuine, and cooperated with him. That year he gained honours.

Once he had matriculated Geoff successfully applied for university entrance. He commenced the first year of a Bachelor of Science degree; part time, studying geology as well because his master in secondary school had once said 'there's oil in the West, we'll find it one day, there's lots of it here!' He believed that going into mineral exploration would enable him to accrue riches enough to become a doctor. He continued in his position as Chemistry Cadet. He became a science representative on the Student Union and began to enjoy his new lifestyle enormously. However, changes were in the air.

Only a month after Geoff had commenced university studies, he spied an advertisement in the West Australian newspaper, for the Empire Air Training Scheme. The British Royal Air Force was seeking Australian young men aged between seventeen and a half and twenty five, to apply for short service commissions, under the scheme. Successful applicants would sign up for a period of four years active list service and six years reserve service, be taken to England to train and serve, then return to their home country with a gratuity of five hundred pounds sterling. That would be enough money to commence a medical degree! With the flying skills he would learn in the RAF, he could go searching for minerals at weekends, to pay for the rest of the course.

Geoff sent off for the application forms. Then the fun began.

Fred Cornish was not prepared to sign. Having been in the First World War, he held enormous reservations about war despite having been awarded the Military Medal. As Geoff was still only seventeen he required his father's permission. Dot colluded with her son by hiding the application documents when they were delivered by the postman.

'But Dad, this is just to apply; it doesn't mean I'll get it. There'll be a lot of people applying. I mightn't even be accepted,' he pleaded.

'What! A son of mine not get it!' Fred snorted.

He signed on the dotted line.

The Scheme was designed for peacetime, and entailed the selection, every six months, of twenty five each, of Australians, New Zealanders, Canadians and South Africans, who might serve anywhere in the world. The pay was seven times what Geoff was then earning. He enquired of the RAF headquarters in Melbourne whether recruits could undertake University studies during their RAF tenure. The answer was in the affirmative. 'They didn't want you to be an officer and a gentleman for six years and then a beach bum off Fremantle for the rest of your life.'

Geoff was shortlisted and the tough selection process began. There were three long interviews, lots of tests including reaction time, a full medical examination, and screening for colour blindness. Mental aptitude and resilience, quick thinking and general level of education were all assessed. Geoff's now impressive academic background would have helped as would his being at the lower end of the required age range because the twenty five year olds were seen as too old. After three weeks of interviews with Senior Black Jack Walker of the RAAF in May, successful applicants were notified in June. Eighty young men applied from Perth and four were selected. The others were Doug Peterkin, a friend from night school, Jack Slatter and Kent Hughes. There were parties and celebrations before the men left.

While researching this book, the author became aware that information from the time was available on the World Wide Web. The records of Geoff's application were there, including the handwritten assessment forms filled out by the personnel who had carried out the interviews. These faded, fascinating documents are reproduced on the following pages.

ROYAL AIR FORCE

NOTE.—No documents must be forwarded with this application.

A.M. FORM 696.

ROYAL AIR FORCE.

Application for Commissioned Service in the Royal Air Force for a period of Four Years Active List Service and Six Years Reserve Service.

Please read these notes before completing the form:—

(a) All questions must be answered in candidate's own handwriting; it is not sufficient to leave the space for reply blank or insert a dash. Incorrect answers may prejudice an applicant's chance of selection.
(b) The certificate on page 3 must be completed. The parent's or guardian's signature must be appended if the candidate is under 21.
(c) When completed this form should be despatched to The Under Secretary of State, Air Ministry (S.7.c.), Kingsway, London, W.C.2.
(d) The submission by an applicant of false or falsified documents in connection with his application may render the applicant liable to prosecution.

(1) Surname (in capitals)	CORNISH
(2) Christian names (in full, in capitals)	GEOFFREY JAMES
(3) Permanent address	15 Joseph St., West Leederville, West Australia
(4) Present address for correspondence, stating date until which it holds good	15 Joseph St., West Leederville, W.A. Permanently
(5) Are you married? (*Note—Candidates must be unmarried at date of entry.*)	no
(6) Date and place of birth	20th June, 1921. Newcastle St., West Perth
(7) Are you of pure European descent?	yes
(8) Nationality (*Full particulars of any change of nationality must be given.*)	australian
(9) Father's name in full, permanent residence, profession, and birthplace (*If deceased, last residence, profession etc., must be stated.*)	Frederick William Cornish, 15 Joseph St., W. Leederville, W.A. Clerk, Government Railways. Ballarat, Victoria.
(a) Mother's maiden name in full and birthplace.	Doris Amelia Blackmore, Perth
(10) (i) Nationality of parents at their birth:— (a) Father (b) Mother (ii) Has either parent acquired any other nationality? (If so, full particulars must be given.)	australian australian

(11) Occupation since leaving school or college. (*This question must be very carefully answered.*)

Approximate dates of employment	Name, address and business of employer	Nature of work on which Candidate has been engaged	Cause of leaving
1-10-35 to 31-1-37	R. G. Lapsley, Yorkshire House, St. George's Tce., Perth. Analytical Chemist	Laboratory attendant	Employer's resignation from business.
1-3-37	Chemistry Dept., University of W.A.	Laboratory attendant (Cadet)	~~Still~~ Still employed

(1151) Wt. 37952-2771 20,000 2/38 T.S. 700
(1003-150) Wt. 21611-1161 21,000 8/38 T.S. 700

INTERVIEW RECORD

R.A.A.F. INTERVIEW FORM (For Cadetships)

Signature of Candidate: .... Name of Candidate: Cornish G.J.

1. Age as at 1.7.39	18½
2. Present (or most recent) occupation:	Laboratory attendant – 18 years – chemistry at Varsity
3. Secondary School:	Perth Tech
4. School examinations passed and scope of education:	Passed Intermediate: Phy., El.Sc. Eng., Arith., Trig., Geom., Alg., Hist., Geog., Chem., Latin, French, Bus. Prince. Leaving. Distinction
5. Technical qualifications:	Nil. Keen on Photography
6. Reasons for wanting to join the Air Force:	Flying & Education
7. Flying or Service experience.	Nil
8. First preference and reason:	R.A.F. or ~~R.A.A.F.~~ Wider experience. Makes these
9. Sport:	Tennis – Swimming.
10. Appearance and manners.	9st 5-6
11. Intelligence, accuracy, general alertness, quickness of observation:	Intelligent type. Alert
12. Personality:	Very Pleasant
13. General promise of fitness for service:	Shows definite promise
14. Medical Interview:	Yes. ~~No.~~ ~~Defer.~~

a bit young.

4

A BEGINNING AT LAST

When the twenty two Australian young men chosen, sailed for Britain on the 20,000 ton *Orama* in August 1939, Geoff Cornish was one of the four who boarded at Fremantle. On 21 August, he was seen off by his very excited family, although no one was more excited than Geoff. His brothers and sister were there, with twelve-year-old Gordon wrapped in a greatcoat to conceal his mumps.

The departure had all the trappings of the era when travel by ocean liner was the only means of reaching the 'old country'. Every family had memories of special departures and homecomings, in this case those of Geoff's father, Fred and his brother Joe, and World War One. Recollections were of sadness, joy, family reunion and the children's fishing day trips using Fred's Railway Gold Pass. It was dark before the ship pulled out and the last that the young men saw of Australia was Rottnest Island lighthouse.

Five days into the voyage, as fear of war gathered pace, the ship was blacked out. The same night they saw for the last time, their emblem the Southern Cross in the sky overhead. Geoff made friends with the purser and first officers and had his first experience of 'hard drinking'. Lots and lots of duty-free beer, in contrast to the odd clandestine ale back in Western Australia, where Fred's standards and a drinking age of twenty one prevailed. Life onboard ship was enjoyable and frivolous initially for the new sailors, on their first real adventure. And what an adventure it was to become. Days and nights of entertainment, talk and alcohol were punctuated by the customary celebrations on crossing the equator and stopping at their first foreign port, Colombo – a feast of sights, smells and sounds. After an exciting day there, life quickly became more serious.

They were now on their way to war. One of the boys heard the British Prime Minister Neville Chamberlain's declaration speech over the ship's radio. He raced to tell the others, took the last eleven stairs in one stride, and broke his ankle. Their first casualty. The same young man – John Crossman – would be one of the first to die, after prophesying his fate in a letter to his sister 'Should this last any time I guess I'll be lucky to see home again'. John regarded himself as a latter day Errol Flynn, modelling his personality on Flynn's, even sporting the appropriate moustache. Another of the Australians described it in his diary as 'a war nobody wants'.

The ship was directed to turn around, head south and recross the equator, proceed to Mombassa to take on board fuel and provisions and sail to the Cape of Good Hope. The original plan to go via the Suez Canal to Aden, the Red Sea, Gibraltar and the Mediterranean, was scuttled. On 3 September 1939 Britain declared war on Germany, a turning point in the young men's lives. Steaming down the East Coast of the African continent, cruising in daylight within sight of land, the *Orama* next stopped at Port Elizabeth. She took aboard provisions, fuel and one would assume, anything which might be required now that this had become a wartime journey. No disembarkations were permitted. On 17 September she berthed at Capetown, a harbour even more crowded than Colombo. Again, no disembarkation was permitted. The liners *City of Benares* and the yellow and white liveried *Strathallan* were there. They now had guns mounted, and within months would become troopships. There were more ships visible than water in Capetown Harbour.

By 19 September the *Orama* was away again, headed for Sierra Leone. Her occupants learned later that in the darkness, the ship passed the famous 'pocket' battleship the *Graf Spee* shortly after it sunk a merchant ship on the same route. History reveals that the *Graf Spee* sunk three ships in that area during September and October – the *SS Clement* on 30 September, the *SS Newton Beech* on 5 October and the *SS Ashlea* on 7 October. They could indeed have passed all three.

Every ship in the Atlantic scurried to Freetown for Royal Navy protection. Here, the passengers were allowed ashore. 'A place you'd never want to go back to.' 'Filthy dirty, smelly, exciting, crowded and so noisy.' They were ferried across on the little boats which hung on the sides of the ship. 'Pat' Macrossan had far too much to drink. He fell overboard and had to be fished out of the water.

All ships were detained at Sierra Leone and directed to sail in guarded convoy. Only three large, speedy liners – the 23 knotters including the *Orama* – were permitted to 'race' ahead. They proceeded in a V formation and zigzagged from Freetown up the West Coast of Africa.

Their last formal dinner on the *Orama* was a celebration. The menu of Crème Montoregueil, poached King Klip, boeuf à la mode, roast haunch of mutton, college pudding and bananas in jelly was followed by coffee in the lounge. The menu cards were signed by every Australian and kept as a memento of the night. Many of the menu cards survive to this day. The boys had prepared a concert of limericks, each tailored to the personality of the 'victim'. The limericks were introduced by: *That was a cute little rhyme, tell us another one do!* sung to the tune of *Here's to the next man to die*. Geoff's limerick went:

Geoff Cornish has come from the west
At reciting he is one of the best
His cobbers are tough
They're hairy and rough
They've sure put him through a stiff test!

The group reached the mist and cloud of Southampton on Friday 13 October, and was whisked quickly to London. The quality and speed of the train trip astounded them: 'The trains in Australia were pups!' Geoff was struck by the 'Incredible rows of tiny chimney pots along the railway line – a little line of four ceramic pots on every chimney' and surprised by the amount of open space. 'We thought that such a small country, with so many people could have no more than an oval here and there.' They entered a blacked out London to be welcomed at Australia House by the Australian High Commissioner and the Press.

'We were so excited! We were so looking forward to our training and our war experience. Fear didn't come into it, not at eighteen.' By the end of 1940, eight of them would be dead.

On the same day as the *Evening Standard* headlined: 'Australian RAF men plot zigzag course here: take 8 weeks,' the *HMS Royal Oak* was sunk at her mooring in the Scapa Flow Harbour of the Orkney Islands. The ship's demise cost 833 lives and she sank in fifteen minutes because her mooring in such a 'safe' harbour had allowed windows and hatches to be open. The boys mused at two disasters befalling Britain on Friday the 13th: her first capital ship loss of the war and the arrival of the twenty two Aussie boys, to help her!

Their first impression of London was incredulity: seeing Buckingham Palace, Trafalgar Square, the institutions with which their childhood memories were crammed. They walked around the town that evening, mentally and physically stimulated, excited by all they saw. They were enthralled by double decker buses, the huge railway stations, escalators, the Underground, impressed with the convenience – the proximity of Australia House to the Air Ministry in Aldwych, and to Savoy House, the home of the Western Australian State Government. They wondered when they would see that great train the *Flying Scotsman*, so familiar from childhood stories. They retired to the Strand Palace Hotel for their first sleep in the new 'old' country. They left next morning for Cambridge to begin their training.

An obstacle emerged before they even left London. RAF officials informed them of a change of plans – a 'typical pommy trick'. Their Commissions had been issued in peacetime – 'Britain is now at war: your previous contracts are invalid!' This meant a drop in standing to Sergeant Pilot – a non-commissioned rank, a decrease in pay, employment only for the duration of war and no gratuity or entitlements on discharge – cancellation of all the conditions which had enticed them to Britain in the beginning. The boys were outraged. Pat Macrossan's father was Chief Justice of Queensland, back home. Pat contacted him in Brisbane and the Judge became their Counsel in the matter. He advised that they had valid contracts which must be honoured:

> If not, they must return you to Australia under arrangements of equal comfort to those granted on your outward passage. You may then join the RAAF as Commissioned Officers.

The RAF caved in completely and quickly as the boys settled into Jesus College and Cambridge.

The antiquity of Cambridge contrasted indelibly with Perth. Perth's centenary was in 1929, when Geoff was eight years old. The young men went punting on the River Cam, shaded by the willow trees along the river bank. Surrounded by pigeons, they walked on the lawns across the river from the College and marvelled at Christopher Wren's architecture and Grumbold's famous bridge.

Whilst quartered in Jesus College they spent two weeks quickly learning the rudiments of life as 'gentlemen' of the RAF. Days were spent 'square bashing', learning rules and practising Morse code. Evenings were spent in Cambridge's wonderful public houses, becoming familiar with the local ales and people. At night they would say they were 'Going back to Jesus'. Their being treated as 'gentlemen' combined with the 'temporary' stamp on their personal files, yielded the designation 'Twenty Two Temporary Gentlemen', which later became the title of a book by Helen Heron, the wife of Jim, one of the twenty two, recording the fate of each of the young men.

By the end of October came time to learn to fly. Geoff and his colleagues moved to Ansty Elementary Flying School, near Coventry in Warwickshire, on 31 October 1939. Ansty had been a civilian flying school, assumed immediately by the RAF once war was declared. Geoff recalled:

> I well remember my first flight in a Tiger Moth – the sheer exhilaration of the ground slipping away and feeling of wind in my hair! I couldn't wait to go solo.

Over two weeks Geoff made ten flights in a Tiger Moth, a total of over seven hours flying time, as the pupil of Flight Lieutenant Knocker and Mr Pegg. The two seater biplane Tiger Moth was the basic pilot trainer aircraft and remains a training and popular private machine to this day. On 13 November, he flew alone. 'A highlight of my life! I revelled in being able to do acrobatics and night flying.'

During the time at Ansty Geoff first made the acquaintance

of the Lady Frances Ryder Scheme and the Bryant family. The Ryder scheme had been established in peacetime to provide hospitality to young men from across the Commonwealth, who took commissions in the RAF. It arranged homestay visits for the men of the dominions, in the homes of the nobility and the gentry.

Geoff and his mate Jim Heron were interviewed by Mrs Bryant and 'Granny' Parkes, who had chosen this title for herself when she became a grandmother at the age of thirty eight. The ladies were then in their sixties. The 'interview' took place in the standard Ryder format – conversation, cakes and afternoon tea. Although the setting was so comfortable, the ladies were skilled and perceptive assessors of their subjects.

Geoff's first visit was to General and Mrs Widdington at Aylesbury, but his trip with Jack McIntosh to the Bryants led to a friendship which would endure and sustain him right through the war, and beyond. Geoff and Jack travelled by train to Stratford on Avon and were met, not by one of the Bryant family but by Jack the Butler, driving a Bentley. The boys were highly impressed. They had a wonderful weekend, learnt the history of the scheme, and soon learned why Mrs Bryant had emphatically requested Australian guests.

Colonel Bryant, of 'Bryant and May' matches' fame, was in retirement from a career as an officer in the Home Guard. Mrs Bryant – this was her second marriage – had formerly been Mrs Westray. Her son, Jim Westray had been a flyer, one of the three involved in the 'Stinson' crash in Australia, on Queensland's Lamington Plateau in February 1937. He was the survivor who crawled almost to safety, but perished nonetheless. Mrs Bryant had visited Australia in 1938 to unveil a plaque in his memory, at the O'Reillys' property in the rugged rainforest mountains of Queensland.

Geoff would regularly spend weekends at the Bryants' full

working farm and manor but sadly not so McIntosh, who drowned while flying Coastal Command Hudsons. When his plane went down in October 1940 the weight of his boots prevented him from swimming to safety, ironically for a man who had been a champion surfer and lifesaver.

The Bryants' home, Goldicote Manor near Alderminster, was resplendent with antiques. Geoff derived particular joy from Colonel Bryant's collection of genuine, original etchings of Heath Robinson inventions which lined the corridor to the gentlemen's lavatory. Geoff's favourite to this day remains a scene of a family at dinner. A butler serves peas to the diners, via a system of mechanical processes entailing his first placing them, via spoon and fork, onto a conveyor. The peas are then gravity-fed to the next of some twenty five processes and are finally delivered directly into the (hopefully open) mouth of each diner. Colonel Bryant was the proud possessor of at least a dozen of the etchings. As an avid and aspiring inventor and improviser himself, Geoff adored these works of art. The Bryants told the young men that they were to regard them as family, and their home as their own, for the duration.

The experiences afforded by participation in the Ryder scheme could only be described as fantastic. Geoff's first stay saw him skating on the iced-over lake of his host. Another visit yielded his first try at a fox hunt. He'd never even seen a wooden stile. He was given a seventeen and a half hand horse – ridiculous for someone of such diminutive stature and no experience – and expected to manage. The horse was so broad that Geoff could not make his splayed knees exert any pressure on the flanks to slow the horse down. He fell at the first fence, which was probably a blessing. He led the horse to a stream, enticed it into the water, then remounted whilst the horse was lower than he. The horse carried him home.

The Ryder scheme was not just an experience, but yet another education. The way the English treated food was an eye opener: a huge dining room with a butler; the main meal in the middle of the day; high tea; pork pies; gorgonzola cheese; pies with whole eggs in them; partridge and grouse.

They went shooting for the aforesaid birds, and hunting. The beagles would sort out the hares, the pointers would deal with the foxes; the boys were given shotguns. A Mr Fox managed the farm!

For the months of December and January Geoff's log book would read like the running sheet for a roller coaster, although the time taken to reach the required hours' flying was a source of frustration for all. It was a savagely cold winter with two feet of snow for five months. By February it was impossible for vehicles to get through the snow into the base to deliver provisions. The curriculum had been completed and the instructors didn't know what to do with their charges. The repetition of work already covered was getting everyone down. The thoroughly bored Australians volunteered to walk the couple of miles in to Walsgrave and carry back the provisions. The offer was welcomed and the excursions became a routine. Trudging through such deep snow in heavy, fur lined flying boots was hard work but their feet stayed warm. The weight of the provisions made progress slow and they quickly learned to transport only a couple of days' goods at a time and bury the rest in the snow until they returned. Initially they would leave eighty percent beneath the snow. This not only made the journeys manageable, but guaranteed the boys many sanctioned absences from class to undertake them. They would progressively move the buried supplies closer, in order to save time which could then be spent having a couple of ales before the walk back. The system served them well, giving respite from boredom and from the company of the more lethargic

Englishmen. It provided exercise and an outing, and best of all it afforded a little local socialisation.

There were many, many days when the weather made it impossible to contemplate flying but nevertheless by April the rookies had enough hours to gain their first licences. On 9 April 1940, after 73 hours and 40 minutes flying, Geoff's log book attested to his proficiency with the Tiger Moth.

Next they went to Cranwell Flying Training School in Lincolnshire, the headquarters of the RAF. Cranwell was not only the location of all significant operations of the RAF but the place where key personnel from all of the Allied Countries would gather. Everything of significance and strategic importance emanated out of Cranwell. All primary institutions were there.

The group arrived at Cranwell on 10 April, during the battle for France. 'France fell while we were there.' Geoff's training was now on Oxfords and from his first flight on 12 April, he quickly advanced to his first solo venture on 17 April.

The *Ox Box*, AS10 Oxford was a multi-engine three-seater advanced trainer monoplane with a speed of 190 mph at 10,000 feet. It enabled training to be given in navigation and direction finding, high-altitude bombing, air gunnery, aerial photography, night-flying and twin-engine flying

This was serious. The men also had significant responsibility for security:

> We had to learn quickly. We were issued with gasmasks. We did duty up the water tower watching for gliders and paratroopers, should they appear during the night. We had one rifle between three of us and no fallback plans.

The aerodrome could never be left unguarded. The home of the RAF was the most obvious of targets. The boys concentrated hard on their tuition, their flying and their navigation studies. They learned to fly by 'visual flying rules' – VFR – because there was at the time no sophisticated equipment, in contrast to later times during the war. Although they had gained confidence and competence in the operation of their aircraft, bringing their machines back after dark was a challenge. 'We had to be able to see an object, to navigate by it'. Night navigation at first seemed impossible. The group gained their 'Wings' on 3 June 1940, seventeen days before Geoff's nineteenth birthday.

The days at Cranwell were happy and fulfilling and while there they were close enough to London to head there for their leave. Being well aware of what might lie ahead of them as airmen, the boys sometimes displayed quite hedonistic behaviours. Having been told that their life expectancy as bomber pilots was six weeks, they determined to pack those weeks to the full.

One occasion Geoff describes as 'The only time we really tangled with the law'. They were in London. 'We'd been to a pub and a nightclub and were really hungry.' There were eight of them in Trafalgar Square. It was 2.00 am and the city was in blackout.

'Fish and chips?'
'Yeah'
'Could take a while to find'
'Let's split up'
'Ok, four pairs'
'We'll meet back here in an half an hour'
'Right'

Too logical. They thought that if they all hit pay dirt they'd have a great feed. If some did, some didn't, they'd share. Their optimism and confidence were well heightened by alcohol. They wandered off and eventually returned. No chips. Only one had found seafood and it was a live crayfish. How to cook it? Their bravado did not extend to eating it raw and wriggling. A more attractive amusement became evident while they pondered what to do:

> 'Look, it walks funny!'
> 'Not as funny as you!'
> 'Let's teach it to go straight!'
> 'Along a line!'
> 'We can make a collar with our shoelaces – tie them altogether, they'll be yards.

The creature was eventually harnessed, placed strategically in the middle of Trafalgar Square, and ordered to march straight. Some time later the crustacean was perceived to be making good progress. The men helped, all down on hands and knees, enthusiastically giving encouragement and direction. 'Come on, you can do it!'

They didn't notice the approach of a paddy wagon. Very soon they were secured for the night, inside what turned out to be Bow Street police station.

Next morning they were greeted by an unamused sergeant, condescension personified:

> 'I realise that you boys are under a great strain, but I really must report this to your Commanding Officer.'
> 'We're not telling you anything' they chorused.

Eventually relenting, they each supplied name, rank and number, which was all the information they were compelled under the terms of the Geneva Convention and permitted under RAF security regulations, to give to anyone. Certainly not squadron number.

> 'We're not telling you anything else!' The sergeant was furious, red faced:
>
> 'We police have our ways and means of finding these things out!' He barked, 'Your Commanding Officer?'
>
> 'Well, you shouldn't have much trouble there, that's him in the next cell!'
>
> 'Get out of here!'
>
> They were never charged.

Such adventures as this were a safety valve. Knowing at nineteen that you probably have no future, is subliminally terrifying and they lived life to the full, every minute. They remained at Cranwell until late July, which for Geoff was some two months after receiving his wings. During this period he learned that he was to be allocated to Bomber Command, (because of his 'performance under responsibility'). 'My fate was decided.' He was attracted to night flying and had applied for it. He was happy with the news. Next came navigation training at St Athan for the group who would go on into Bomber Command.

5

TRAINED, TRIED AND TRUE

From late July, for a month at St Athan, Geoff flew almost daily. Navigation training flights in Avro Ansons appeared in his log book from 30 July until 30 August 1940. The Avro Anson or *Faithful Annie* – cold, slow and noisy – was the most famous British aircrew trainer of all time, and although outclassed once war began was retained as a patrol boat over the Channel until the Oxford became available in large numbers.

St Athan is located on the northern arm of the Bristol Channel, on the coast of southern Wales, west of Cardiff and Barry. Ideally located for navigational training, it provided immediate access to inland Britain, the sea, and entry to the whole south east sweep of the continent. Its position made German access difficult, requiring aerial intruders to either fly across Britain or go a lengthy route via the Irish Coast.

Life on the St Athan air base was cosmopolitan, most of all at this time. The Battle of Britain occurred whilst the men were there and the base housed the 'remnants of the Continental Air Forces'. There were Polish, French, Belgian, Czech and many Dutch airmen. When France fell, everything that could fly was directed to the huge St Athan airbase. The new men from the Continental Allied Countries underwent further flying training and then flew with the RAF, increasing the numbers and extending the repertoire of skills of the British Force. The Europeans also brought detailed local knowledge of the terrain into which the squadrons were flying daily.

The international flyers trained in the same squadrons, ate in the same mess, enjoyed the same companionship and participated in the same leisure activities as their hosts. The native English speakers practised their schoolboy French and generally got on well with the newcomers, with some like Geoff taking the opportunity to learn the rudiments of any language on offer. Employing one's immature linguistic skills became a challenge, which would be exploited whenever possible, throughout the war.

Leaders from the occupied European countries would visit, to encourage their men and boost their morale and camaraderie. Ex-President Benez of Czechoslovakia – a tiny man in jodhpurs – was a regular visitor at lunch and would as often sit with the RAF men as with his own countrymen. Bob Vanderstock was there, a Dutchman who would reappear and become a leader in Stalag Luft III. Although these men had lost their rank and lost their country, they hadn't lost their uniform. General de Gaulle visited. Prince Bernhard of the Netherlands was a 'regular', and had meals with his men to boost their spirits.

Although the boys recognised that they were living in interesting times, they had no idea how significant a part of history it would turn out to be.

Bombings frequently occurred around the base while they were in their navigation classes: 'We'd dive under the desks, count the bangs. Always four.' After the fourth they'd get up from the floor, dust off and get on with the lesson. 'You'd know whether it was a Heinkel or whatever, from the tone of the engines.' Afterwards, if there was time, they'd go outside and see where the bombs had landed and what damage they'd done. 'It was part of the lesson, part of the life, every day.'

A first hand experience of German interference, Geoff's earliest, dramatic instance of action, was during a reconnoître in an Avro Anson on 16 August. It was a typical exercise, with Geoff as navigator to Flight Lieutenant McKinley, an Australian, RAAF flyer. The exercise was to cross over the Isle of Man, circle over the east coast of Ireland and back along the Bristol Channel to base without landing. As the aircraft moved along the Channel, Geoff noticed something in the water below them: 'there's a periscope down there,' he said.

The captain looked. 'Yes, better report it to base.' Geoff plotted their position, and the wireless op sent a signal back. After about ten minutes the operator called to the pilot. 'Return and shadow enemy submarine. Await further orders.'

'Reality!' Geoff rejoiced, 'we're following a moving target!'

They had just learned about moving targets, in class, and now had the opportunity to navigate around one. They slipped back towards the intruder and stayed behind it, hovering like a little angry moth. At last a big Sunderland flying boat from South Wales, was alerted and arrived. It kept cruising as McKinley's 'plane became low on fuel and time and had to return to base. They heard no more about the Sunderland, never found out whether he dropped anything. They were the toast of the town that evening.

Geoff was proud of his navigation skill which he attributed to his lifelong love of precision. The discipline of his learning to time resuscitation and photography led logically into the requirements of navigation.

Following the period at St Athan, Geoff and his colleagues were posted to Upper Heyford Operational Training Unit in Oxfordshire, to gain experience in the specific aircraft which they would fly on their squadron. Here, their Flight Commander was Squadron Leader Augustus 'Gus' Walker. Gus had been with Oxford University Air Squadron before the war and was an accomplished airman. Geoff would record his first 45 minute operational flight from this base, in Anson no 5018, on 17 September as a second pilot. At twenty eight, Gus was nearly a decade older than most of his pupils. A scholar by background, Gus was exceptionally good at theory and a great teacher. He had played rugby, a brilliant fly half for England. He was the quintessential sportsman and a real 'man's man'. The boys would do anything for him. Gus enquired whether Geoff had played 'football' and Geoff was able to say that he had, thanks to 'Pud' Smallwood, back at school. Thereafter, in addition to flight training, Gus engaged Geoff in rugby. After the day's programme they'd adjourn. 'Be on the field at 5!' 'Yes, Sir!' Gus would tell Geoff to give him a pass. 'Again! Again!' Six feet behind, two feet behind. 'Again!' At the end of the hour the trainee was 'absolutely buggered'.

September 17 to 26 saw further intensive training on Ansons and at last Geoff's log book recorded two hundred total flying hours. Next he would progress to Bristol Blenheims, Handley Page Herefords with an in-line engine, and Hampdens which were the same basic aircraft as the Hereford but with a radial engine. There were many instances of bombing operations amongst those logbook entries. He was destined to mainly fly Hampdens and on 12 October, Geoff recorded his first flight with Guy Gibson, in Hampden no 2114, in the apprentice role of second pilot. Guy, already the holder of a Distinguished Flying Cross, quickly became Geoff's favourite and most memorable teacher.

Guy had returned to the Training Unit after two full tours without a break, a full 67 missions. He completed a whole year of bombing operations. He had applied for transfer to Fighter Command in order to escape the mandatory six months in an Operational Training Unit (OTU) after his first tour. Later in the war the pinnacle of his success would be leading the famous Dam Busters raid on the Ruhr valley.

When Gibson was posted to Upper Heyford and was driving from there to Scampton, his car was caught in heavy snow in the Pennines. He telegraphed: 'Delayed, bad weather, arriving Monday evening'. Signed Gibson, DFC. His superior, Group Captain Vincent who had risen from Marine ranks, was unamused. Gibson was soundly carpeted for his 'non-cooperation'.

Guy was of similar height to Geoff, blond haired, blue eyed: 'We got on so well together.' He became an immediate role model.

Although Geoff asserts that there was no conscious hero status at the time, Guy Gibson and Gus Walker clearly became Geoff's heroes. Guy loved life, had a lovely girlfriend, Eve, whom he flew off to marry in Cardiff that November. 'Guy was such a good teacher,' Geoff explains:

> Whenever we were in the air he was the perfect instructor. He would tell me where to look, how to observe, how long to look in certain directions, how long to go on a steady course, how frequently to break to get away from searchlights or stop the night fighters getting us. How far you could take an aircraft in a dive, what were the supposed limits, how far you could stretch them. He took them well beyond their limit. He taught me how to do that, how to handle the aircraft when it was beyond the supposed limit. Everything he taught me stood me in good stead, because there were occasions when I was in great danger. His teaching became automatic. I learnt it and thought 'thanks Guy, for that'. He was always instructing. His style of flying was excellent. I know that I owe my life to Guy's tuition even though I was with him only a few weeks.

On 15 October, while Geoff was flying with Guy, the Irish Army captain in charge of anti aircraft defence on the base, wished to be flown to Belfast from whence to travel south, home to Dublin, for his leave.

Neither Guy nor Geoff had been to Belfast and were happy to take a Hereford and assist. When they reached Belfast, the Irishman invited them for a drink. Assuming he meant a drink in a hut on the base, the men stayed in uniform. They squeezed into a little Hillman Ute 'jeep', breathed in, and were taken into Central Belfast. Many people were milling around. The Luftwaffe had bombed the city the previous night.

The locals thought they were Germans! The passenger door flew open. 'Get out you Nazi bastards!'

One mob held the Irishman, another grabbed Gibson and lifted him up by his elbows. Guy realised they were in trouble. 'Show 'em your wings!' he shouted to Geoff who obliged, flinging his coat front open.

'You've even got RAF uniforms as well, come out you Nazi bastards! Filthy spies in British uniforms!' They wanted to string them up. Things were not looking good.

The Irishman let fly in Gaelic and the attackers calmed down. Geoff and Guy had a couple of drinks and returned to their 'plane.

The early bomber pilots had a steep learning curve and only the very best and most fortunate survived. Geoff recalls: 'You were basically stepping straight into dead men's shoes. We went into war quickly, because men were being killed every day'. Geoff desperately wanted to be posted to the Hampden, 106 Squadron from which Guy had come, but that was not possible. He was to go to 50 Squadron, based at Lindholme, near Doncaster in early November 1940, just after the end of the Battle of Britain. His log book declares his skills to be of a high standard – 'The makings of a good captain' – continuing ironically 'but for his small experience in Hampdens'. Many, many young men were later recognised as having been sent out on operations with pitifully short periods of experience in the aircraft in which they flew. Relatively speaking, Geoff's hours were considerable.

Although he was excited to be going to a squadron, Geoff was sorry to leave the training unit and the inspiration and comradeship of Guy and Gus. They in turn lamented the good fortune of the boys who were moving on to squadrons while they were 'stuck in Training Command'.

Five weeks after arriving at Lindholme, Geoff learned that the squadron was to have a new Commanding Officer, Wing Commander Walker. Sure enough it was Gus, and Geoff was one of the few men who'd known him in Training Command. The friendship and the rugby training resumed.

Gus was always on the runway when crews departed and returned. He shunned the use of a military vehicle and rode his old bicycle. Up and down the runway, tin hat on his head and gas mask slung across his shoulder, to bob up and down as he pedalled. Gus personally waved off every flight, always waited until every last one had gone. Every return was likewise greeted by a wave and a salute.

'Gus was the last man I saw on the tenth of April, when I left on my last journey,' Geoff remembers. 'He was a great man, one of the best'.

When Geoff joined 50 Squadron in November 1940, he was posted as Second Pilot – a bit of a misnomer because a Hampden is so narrow that only one person sitting can put their elbow on each side of the aircraft. They called it the 'flying suitcase' or the 'flying tadpole'. It had a long narrow tail, with the main body of the aircraft resembling a suitcase. The Handley Page Hampden was a twin-engined, mid-wing, medium bomber with twin fins and rudders. Its 3 foot (one metre) wide fuselage was known to be assembled in two pieces and joined together after all its equipment had been installed.

This craft had notorious accident rates and was eventually used mainly for mine laying and leaflet dropping over the occupied countries such as Holland. Leaflet dropping was a common activity for familiarisation with enemy terrain, practice flights and had the additional benefit of attempting to cheer the residents of the occupied territory.

In the Hampden the pilot was up top in the front, the second pilot was at the front but right down in the nose of the aircraft. Perspex windows surrounded him and he could see out clearly but could neither see nor handle the controls. Second pilot was navigator, bomb aimer and front gunner, if and when he ever had a chance to attack the ground. He could communicate with the pilot by standing up, turning 180 degrees, and stretching his hand forward to tap the pilot on the foot. 'Second' had the best view of anybody, albeit along with such a formidable suite of duties. As navigator, he had to be always supremely alert. There were none of the more sophisticated mechanisms or methods of navigation available that would be developed later in the war. The only way was good old VFR. This required absolutely careful, continual, and accurate map reading. 'I enjoyed it. I love that sort of thing,' Geoff says. The requirement for absolute precision, accompanied by the stimulation of being the first to see every bit of action, excited and utterly captivated him.

Much of Geoff's time as Second Pilot was to George Weston, a New Zealander, whom he describes as: 'A darned good pilot and a very good skipper'. George said later that he was sad to see Geoff's promotion to captaincy, because they had worked so well together. George and his friend Canadian Jimmy Whitecross both received their DFCs at the same time that Geoff was promoted. There was quite a celebration.

Given that the duties and responsibilities of second pilot had been nothing to do with piloting at all meant that it was a big change when one took command. Geoff found the new role:

> Different, exciting, memorable. I was so glad of the responsibility. It was so exciting. I just couldn't help myself, I was bursting with pride.
>
> I remember the feeling, the thrill of being in charge. Not really a good word 'crew'. Crew really means the ranks downward, but it was never that, always just a plain team, each with a job to do. They bossed me around with friendly banter.
>
> I remember once coming back from a long trip. Suddenly over the intercom, 'ttttttttt'.
>
> 'What's wrong?'
>
> 'Christ it's cold up here, I'm freezing! Why don't we go down where it's a bit warmer, and have a go at those searchlights?'
>
> Then the second one's teeth started chattering, and then the whole three of them.
>
> 'All right' I agreed, and we had a go at hitting the islands off the Dutch Coast.

Early in the war Hampdens were being used in daylight bombing along the French canals, and suffered tremendous casualties. Throughout this time, aircraft losses far exceeded the pace at which replacements could be manufactured.

When Geoff joined the squadron there was one target outstanding – it was very long range and impossible to reach from Lindholme. The objective was to blow up the Italian submarines – a task which had already been unsuccessfully attempted many times – in Bordeaux, awaiting repairs after the Royal Navy had clobbered them in the Atlantic. The Italian submariners loved Bordeaux – beautiful countryside, lots of red wine, good food and pretty girls.

They were taking an inordinate time to get their ships repaired. The Germans had become quite testy about this and word came through from the French underground that unless the Italians moved on by the following Thursday the Germans would simply push them back out into the Atlantic.

It was decided that as their exercise on 14 February 1941, Geoff's squadron would go down and lay mines along the Gironde estuary, departing from St Eval in Cornwall. The Gironde was quite shallow, with a very narrow, deep channel down the middle. The channel was continually dredged and on either side of that channel, the river was only six or eight feet deep. The tactic was to go in very, very high and quietly, cut motors and glide. It was a full moon, pretty dangerous, and the flyers had to be able to identify exactly where to drop the mine, in the deep central channel. They would drop the mine accurately by parachute, as slowly as possible, to prevent it blowing up on impact. If it dropped in shallow water the explosion would blow off the tail of the aircraft. Perfect navigation was required. The pilot would throttle the motors right back until they were just gliding, and on approaching the straight stretch of river the aimer would drop the mine from a height of between 100-150 feet. When the mine aimer said 'mine's gone' the pilot would apply full throttle and head out to sea. If the Germans realised what was happening, they'd come up from the river and defend. The Germans' anti aircraft fire was capable of going from the ground up to about five thousand feet, in a 'box' along the river. They knew that the attacker had to be somewhere in that box and would press all of the triggers at once, in what was called a 'box barrage'. On this occasion Geoff's plane was hit and only just managed to limp back to St Eval. 'That was a very hairy raid.'

They would need means other than their own aircraft to get back to Lindholme. The orders were: 'just bring your parachutes and your crew up by train'. Geoff and the crew set off by train. They travelled on Great Western Railways – GWR – to London then had to change lines to get back up to Doncaster. That meant a tube ride for some miles across London. The boys were very conspicuous in full flying kit, carrying their parachutes.

The Londoners pressed them: 'Come for a drink. We insist.' Geoff acquiesced: 'OK, be back here in two hours!'

The Londoners brought the crew back about half an hour after the train left. The next train was four hours later: 'Be back by then!' This went on for twenty four hours.

Before Geoff managed to round up his men, he was one of the casualties himself. 'We eventually got back to Doncaster and out to the squadron, but that's one raid that I remember well.'

Another memorable trip was attempting to bomb the 32,700 ton *Scharnhorst* in daylight. 'I think that was one of the closest to suicide that we ever had.' The second closest was the one at Brest. 'I landed at Charmy Down, after that one. I got battered pretty badly. They told me to go to St Athan for repairs and to rejoin operations at Charmy Down.' By now Geoff and his mate Jack Ratcliffe as second pilot were an established team.

6

In the Bag

Easter Thursday, 10 April 1941, had been a clear spring day. The men were excited about another operational trip under a full moon. Geoff Cornish was again in command and Jack Ratcliffe second pilot. Briefing was finished and the boys were talking amongst themselves. 'Almost five months of ops,' Geoff noted to himself, poring over his logbook. They went over the flight plan, reiterating where they would leave England and where they would cross onto the continent. Again in their usual Hampden, AD 789 which had always brought them home, albeit sometimes after a hiding. The Hampden's cruising speed of 270 kilometres per hour, top speed of 409 and range of just over 3000 kilometres could comfortably manage the trip to Düsseldorf with its 4000 pound bombload. He knew that it was technically capable of 'catching and overtaking the superior [lighter, faster but lower range] Messerschmitt Bf 110'.

They were clear how long the trip should take – about seven hours, all being well, crossing over Eindhoven and then straight down to Düsseldorf. Drop a load and back home for Easter.

Gus followed them onto the runway as usual astride his bicycle, mask flying, waving the first crew to leave and watching for Dave Powell to follow. These brave little Hampden tadpoles really did look vulnerable, as they slipped up into the night sky.

As the aircraft with its full payload at 20,000 feet moved across Holland, something was different. It was eerie. They were flying in complete darkness – no searchlights, no night-fighters, no anti aircraft fire. This never happened over enemy territory. 'Spooky,' Geoff mused. He didn't know that the Luftwaffe was planning to take full advantage of the brilliantly moonlit night, despite the fact that the RAF was doing the same. Suddenly, an arrow of pale light seemed to be pointing the path to Düsseldorf, moving ahead of the Hampden. The first beam concentrated straight along the ground, then suddenly rolled upwards, striking the Hampden's underbelly, following it as it moved forward. The dazzling blue light was quickly joined by dozens more, from every direction. An array, not a few but hundreds, coordinated in their focus, streaming like ribbons on a maypole. They fixed on the plane as it dived and turned, trying in vain to escape. 'How many, fellas?' Geoff shouted to his crew. 'Ten there, twenty there . . .' Hundreds, they believed. The plane slipped and twisted, with no hope of escaping the cone of light. Diving away from one beam simply plunged the tadpole into the path of twenty more. 'All of Guy's lessons came back to me, but this time nothing would work.'

Only seconds later the first night fighter surged close, incendiary cannons blazing. Close enough to touch, the Messerschmitt 110 thudded through, revealing the black crosses on his undercarriage, pulling out at the last possible second. Another slipped in as the first disappeared. Then a third. Non stop action. They'd got the Hampden's intercom. Geoff was unharmed, protected by the armourplate which shielded his back, head and seat. Not so the crew, who did not have armourplate protection; they had to be able to move around as much as possible and do things, in the tiny tadpole. A tap of the second pilot's hand to Geoff's foot on the rudder bar alerted him to Jack's blood spattered note: 'He's got me'. Cannon fire continued.

There was a drill that if anything happened to the skipper – if he was wounded or incapacitated – he had to call over the intercom for the second pilot to come and replace him. They then would scramble over the main spar, behind and underneath the captain, lower his armour plate, get the back of his seat down flat, and either help him or walk him out of the cockpit. The pilot would have put the aircraft into automatic control. After hauling him backwards, the replacement pilot would clamber over him into place and put the armour plate up. The others took care of the skipper while the second pilot flew the plane. That would not be possible tonight, or ever. Geoff was on his own.

Knowing that Jack Ratcliffe had been badly hurt or he would not have written the note, Geoff realised that his third and fourth men must be injured or dead. The third he could see, on turning round, to be slumped and motionless in his harness. Fire would have had to go straight through the others to have hit Jack and reach Geoff's armour flap.

Then it all happened.

Geoff remembers only the deafening roar, not the explosion – a noise like hammers banging the inside of a water tank. Holes all around, the canopy gone, freezing air rushing all around him. He tried to head for home. He could not control the aircraft. 'I can't function, I've got no navigator, jettison the bombs.' Safe jettison was a requirement over Holland and required reaching out for the toggle. As his hand extended, the toggle disappeared, blown off by a blast of cannon from the latest attacker. The aircraft began to tumble, and the next he knew, he was hanging from a parachute. Whilst severely dazed, he had pulled the ripcord and opened the 'chute. Reflexes and training had done their job.

He had no idea where he was. As he fell, his mate Dave Powell came into view, now also trapped by the searchlights. Dave and his crew had taken off 30 seconds after Geoff. 'Look out Dave, the bloody Messerschmitts!' Geoff screamed from his dangling lines, as one does in a nightmare. As he watched, Dave's plane too succumbed to the incendiaries and burst into flame. Geoff could clearly see only the tracer shells, every tenth cannon. Sixty years later Geoff would learn that he had in fact been the survivor of a Messerschmitt 110 collision, on a night which lost five Hampdens.

Records have revealed that:

> On the night of 10/11 April 1941 the German night fighters took full advantage of the brilliant moonlight and shot down five Hampdens X.3066, X3148, X3153, AD789 and AD828 all of which were operating against Düsseldorf. Bf 11OC-4 serial number 3300 collided with a Hampden and both aircraft crashed near each other at Neer in Holland. The German pilot, Lieutenant H Reese of I/N.1G1, although wounded, managed to bale out but his wireless operator Unteroffizier W Roitzaak was killed. AD789 does seem to be the candidate for this dubious honour.

Geoff was freezing, hurting, disoriented, stunned – seriously affected by the absence of oxygen at altitude. He tried to work out what he could do to help himself land, having no idea what distance away the ground might be. All the daytime training in the world was lost when you had to land at night, in unknown territory, unable to see a thing. Concentrating hard, he eventually managed to manoeuvre towards a piece of clear ground. Hitting the surface hard, in the little patch between trees on three sides and a canal on the fourth, he gradually managed to stand. He was clearly injured but his attention was not to be distracted. He stumbled, hauled in his parachute, wriggled out of the harness and made for the woods. His ankle ached, his head was hurting. He took a few steps and halted, by what felt like metal netting. Turning, he tried another direction, another net. A third change of direction led him to stumble over a sort of box. Kaaa, ck, ck, ck. White hens surrounded him.

A boy of about twelve appeared, opened the gate, and led Geoff to the farmhouse. The family bathed and bandaged his wounds. The father, Mr Mertens, a schoolmaster and the eldest daughter, Wilhelmina, spoke excellent English. He learned that the townspeople watched the sky every night for aircraft and often saw British craft heading for Germany. On the night the Dutch call *White Thursday* they had seen Geoff's plane as soon as it was struck by the searchlights. They watched the burning craft fall from the sky, followed minutes later by a figure hanging from a parachute. This would trigger the townspeople to run and look for the person, to render what help they could. On such evenings the town would be alive with people and the Gestapo would always arrive quickly. The boy who reached Geoff was Martin, who took him across the village to his home. The family warned Geoff that the Gestapo would come. He heard from the other people milling around, that if he did not give himself up they might be taken captive for harbouring him. Geoff recalls his parachute being rescued and hidden, he thought for the girls to make silk underwear.

Wilhelmina managed to remove Geoff's shoes and bathe his injured foot. Sixty years later she remembers the injury: 'It was your foot, you couldn't walk. It was bleeding. The whole village came to have a look at the Australian pilot. We liked him.'

The first of the Gestapo arrived on motorcycles. Lodging machine guns firmly in each of Geoff's kidneys and pressing a pistol to his forehead, they issued the statement familiar to every captive: 'For you, the war is over.' Geoff agreed with them. It certainly looked that way, and he privately hoped that it was only the war that was over. 'I'm generally a pretty agreeable sort of a chap,' he still says.

He was taken to a lockup at Eindhoven airport and secured for the night. Next morning, Good Friday, when he was allowed out into the cobbled courtyard for exercise, he met Dave Powell's crew. Dave had not survived. The reverse outcome of Geoff's night of combat. For the first time, he became a fatalist, could not see how a 'God' could be loving or fair. He and Dave had departed Britain only seconds apart, he was alive, his friend was dead. Killed by the very same German fighters as his three crew. The captives were taken in a black Mercedes to gaol in Amsterdam where they spent the rest of Easter. Many years later when Geoff read the story of Anna Frank, he was sure that he had been in the same gaol and possibly the same room – the description was identical. He was unable to finish reading 'The Diary' and even in the next millennium, remains unable to do so.

On Easter Monday the prisoners were taken by rail down the Ruhr valley to the central Transit Camp, Dulag Luft, in the woods beyond Frankfurt. As the young men travelled down the valley, they were disappointed and astonished to see the city of Cologne almost intact. They had all, including Geoff, carried out bombing operations along that strip and had been led to believe that the city was in ruins.

On arriving at Dulag, Geoff was interrogated extensively, although it would probably have been obvious that such a youthful and relatively junior officer was unlikely to be privy to much in the way of strategic intelligence. His stay there lasted about a month, during which time he met Jimmy Buckley and the famous Roger Bushell.

Geoff's brother Gordon remembers the news coming through of Geoff's crash. The family did not know whether he was alive or dead. Gordon recalled:

> I was home with some sickness or other; I think it was shingles. The postman came and my mother opened the letter and burst into tears. Then she phoned Dad.

His sister Audrey remembers her mother's reaction making headlines. The West Australian newspaper read:

> *Perth Mother's faith: I won't believe he's dead!*

The family do not recall how long it was before they knew that Geoff was alive, and in a manner of speaking, safe.

7

Apprentice kriegie

Dulag Luft, outside Frankfurt am Main, was the staging or transit camp where captured airmen were first incarcerated. Dulag Luft is a contraction of Durchgangslager der Luftwaffe – transit camp for Air Forces. The site was a former agricultural station. All captive aircrew, of every nationality, were kept together in 'Luft' camps and supervised by guards from the same arm of the services. As at Cranwell, almost all the allied countries were represented. The practice of keeping 'like with like' would in later days, be of great benefit to the prisoners and considerable frustration to their custodians.

Each man spent the first few days in solitary confinement while the Luftwaffe interrogators hoped to wring significant information from them. The prisoners stuck firmly to their orders and the Geneva Convention, and revealed only 'name, rank and number'.

After his period in 'solitary', Geoff was allowed to proceed to the open camp. There he met the British 'permanent staff', a group of senior and experienced prisoners. These included Harry 'Wings' Day, Roger Bushell, Jimmy Buckley and Mike Casey. 'Wings' had been appointed Senior British Officer – SBO – and was highly particular about observance of Convention protocols. The 'permanent staff' performed a liaison role between the prisoners – known as 'kriegies' – and the guards, in order to reduce the guards' workload and perhaps maintain a more manageable population of prisoners.

'Wings' Day was aged forty one on capture. Born in Borneo, he was educated in England and served with distinction in the Marine Light Infantry in World War One. He then travelled the world with the marines and transferred to aviation in 1924. He commenced as Commanding Officer of 57 Squadron in 1939. He had been shot down on Friday, 13 October 1939. Wings and Geoff shared the experience of surviving their crews. Day's nickname derived from the anniversary 'Wings Day' not from his commission.

Mike Casey was also born in the colonies and educated in Britain. He applied for a Short Service Commission shortly before war commenced and after what the newspapers described as an 'aerial steeplechase' was shot down near Emden. He and his crew waved to the pilot of their German aggressor after they were safely on the ground. Jimmy Buckley had served on an aircraft carrier pre-war and was shot down while strafing over Calais.

Roger Bushell was born in South Africa, educated there and in England and later at Cambridge. He had commenced study in engineering but became a barrister. He was a European ski champion, known for his formidable speeds and had a sinister scar above his eye, from a skiing accident. In 1932 he joined the 'Millionaires' Squadron,' No 601 of the RAF and later 92 Squadron where his Hurricane caught fire duelling with Messerschmitt 110s. Landing in what he believed was friendly territory, he lit a cigarette and was promptly captured.

The above individuals were purged from Dulag Luft only after the discovery of the first tunnels which was quite early in the war, but after Geoff's departure. That venture was in fact the first attempt at a 'major' escape. It included Roger Bushell, and alerted the Germans to tighten their formerly somewhat moderate security measures. The remaining 'permanent staff' were kept at Dulag until it was closed down in Autumn 1942. Dulag Luft was the location of Geoff's first exposure to tunnelling, although he did not participate in the work at that time.

In late May 1941 Geoff was transferred to Stalag Luft I, a permanent camp at Barth. Barth was located on the Baltic Sea between Stettin and the southern tip of Denmark, some 800 kilometres north-east. 'Stalag' is short for Stammlager or 'common prison' although 'Oflag' would have more correctly described a prison for officers. The term 'Stalag' was used for all of these camps. Adding 'Luft' became the differentiating term and 'Stalag Luft' became the designation of the permanent, prisoner of war camps for captured airmen.

Barth's location near the sea and the unoccupied countries, made escape seem more of a possibility to the prisoners than it did in the other camps. They could sometimes even see yachts out on the sea, from the camp. The discerning feature of the location was that it was absolutely freezing. 'Desolate, flat, windswept and godforsaken – I have goose pimples just thinking about it!' Geoff recalls.

Geoff was to be at Barth for a year and initially shared a room with Jock Patterson and Tommy Guest. Jock had been shot down in a Wellington and Tommy in a Hurricane Fighter. In this room, Geoff had his first wartime experience of 'losing his cool'. None of the men had ever before lived cheek by jowl in such crowded conditions and arguments broke out. Geoff ended up involved in fisticuffs with both Jock and Tommy! No doubt being the type of character selected for air service – intelligent, confident, decisive, and who, in the RAF were seldom challenged or questioned – contributed to the young men's initial difficulty in learning to live amicably in such circumstances. Geoff recalls:

> We were all in our teens; we'd never been cooped up, let alone together. If you disagreed with one bloke and he persisted in saying something that you didn't like, you tended to try and bop him on the nose to shut him up. I got into two fights, just in our room!

Clearly, this situation was not sustainable and Geoff quickly learned to sublimate. Not so all of the men. There were instances related later where individuals broke down under the stress, leading in some cases to suicide. Geoff remembers:

> It was only a lot later I realised that looking after the health of the men in camp was a big concern for the senior officers . . . they appreciated that encouraging meaningful activity and occupation would prevent the men with time on their hands from having fights.

At Barth Geoff made his first acquaintance with the German security staff, known to the men as 'goons' or 'ferrets'. All guards were 'goons'; those who searched for tunnelling activity, often by crawling under buildings and into roofs, were 'ferrets'.

The term 'goon' was one viewed curiously by the guards, who never really succeeded in determining its origin and meaning. When asked, the men would give an explanation which revolved around an abbreviation such as 'German officer or non commissioned officer', but it was more closely related to comic strip characters who were 'low browed, primitive apemen, strong and stupid' and found in London's Daily Mirror newspaper.

The system of nicknames was derived from the long established traditions of British schoolboys and the customs of the first war. The names enabled the prisoners to speak about an individual guard without being understood. They also assisted easy identification of those guards whose names the men found virtually unpronounceable. A soubriquet might be derived from the persons' name, from their physical appearance or from their behaviour.

Hence the most senior guard Lagerfeldwebel Hermann Glemnitz became Dimwits, which did not reflect his personality in the least. Glemnitz was an interesting man – conscientious to a fault, intelligent, observant and in possession of a fine sense of humour. A First World War infantryman and pilot, he had between the wars undertaken work which took him to South America and the US, South Africa and Spain and had lived for a time in Yorkshire. By the beginning of World War Two he was quite wealthy and owned a block of flats in his home town of Breslau. Glemnitz was chief guard, in charge of all the ferrets, security and of course the 'cooler'. He oversaw the distribution of Red Cross parcels and it has been said that none were ever tampered with. Glemnitz spoke excellent English and the prisoners respected him as a truly professional soldier.

Rubberneck – Corporal Karl Griese – was named for his straight Prussian bearing, the long neck which went absolutely vertically from the tip of his head to his chest and back, fore and aft, and his ability to rotate said neck around the most unlikely of corners. Griese was the leader of the 'investigating' ferrets, and delighted in donning his boilersuit and crawling under buildings and into roof cavities. He pursued his work with a passion and was utterly humourless; he disliked and was loathed by the prisoners. Keen Type was the personification of his moniker, and 'Adolph' of course resembled the Fuehrer.

One guard who became important to the prisoners was Hauptman Hans Pieber, who seems not to have had a pseudonym. An Austrian, he had been a recipient of an earlier Nazi honour, which he later renounced. He did not regard himself as German. His disposition, personalty and sympathetic behaviour saw him liked by the kriegies whom he later helped immensely.

A number of these guards would appear in more than one camp and in some instances they would be moved concurrently with the prisoners whom they already knew well.

In Stalag Luft I at Barth, Tommy Guest gave Geoff a moniker which would last a lifetime. Our hero was small, slim, with curly blonde hair and dimples. Not an easy load to carry in the blokey world of the services. Guest was reading a book with endplates depicting little cherubs blowing into the sails of ships crossing the ocean from the old to the new world. He exclaimed: 'look at him, that's him – the cherub in the picture!' It stuck. Although diminishing somewhat when the war was over, 'Cherub' still occasionally resurfaces even in Geoff's eighties.

Geoff soon discovered that Paul Royle, an old friend from Perth who had joined the Empire Scheme in March 1939, was also in the camp. Their parents had been keeping in touch after their sons' departure and would hopefully know by now that both were in captivity, together and at least alive. He arranged to move into Paul's room. Royle and his roommates Joe Hill and Tom 'Piglet' Whiting had commenced digging a tunnel, the mouth of which was under Paul's bed. This provided Geoff's first taste of tunnelling. 'I was small, very fit, didn't have claustrophobia so I got to do a lot of the digging. I dug like fury.'

Barth was situated on heavy clay, slow to dig, most easily cut by using a knife. The ground was frozen, cold, often pure ice and the water table was high. After digging only five or six feet the men would be inundated with freezing, dirty water. These tunnels however, unlike those in the later camps, didn't require shoring up as the firmness of the clay fulfilled that function, especially when frozen in winter. Stalag Luft I provided the opportunity to learn tunnelling and associated skills which would be refined and used to benefit in later situations. The physical effort of the work kept the men's bodies fit and tired, and displaced energies which might otherwise have found more destructive outlets. The activity gave a purpose and routine to daily life.

The prisoners dug several tunnels during their internment at Barth, all of which were eventually found by the ferrets. One was found when a metal rod, salvaged from a window frame to poke up out of the snow and provide air into the tunnel, was detected by one of the guards' Alsatian dogs. The dog smelt human odour in the steam emanating from the piece of pipe but the men managed on that occasion to avoid being sprung. 'I can still see that steam,' Geoff says. After that they kept a vigil by placing a deck chair over the outlet and taking turns to sit there and read.

Tunnelling was of course not the only productive activity. When the men arrived in a camp they were each assigned a duty. If one had a preference, it could often be accommodated. Geoff had enjoyed cooking since first helping his mother as a small boy, and could quickly see the advantage for himself, of looking after the food. He quickly offered to cook and was accepted. Although the prisoners' official rations were cooked in the central kitchen, they were usually inedible. The men virtually relied on food from their Red Cross parcels supplemented by potatoes and sauerkraut. 'We learned a lot from the Poles about potatoes,' he says today. Geoff's upbringing in the Cornish family during the Depression continued to serve him well. He remained a cook for the whole four years in prison camps. 'Because I was the cook I didn't ever have to do the vegetable peeling, the washing up or any of the other chores – and that suited me just fine.' Further justifying his stance he says: 'Someone who couldn't cook might have ruined the food of a dozen or more prisoners!'

Two of the men from Geoff's first year in camps would later become highly significant and many more would become long-term friends and companions. Tommy Guest became the tailor in charge of the group who made outfits for the 'Great Escape', altering all the clothing the men could procure into items that would be required for life 'outside'. Roger Bushell, whom he met briefly in Dulag Luft, would become Big X, the mastermind and chief of operations for the Great Escape from Stalag Luft III.

X–X–X–X–X–X–X

In these camps, captives from nations who were not Geneva Convention signatories, were treated abominably. Russians were universally used as slave labour. Geoff's memory of the treatment delivered to the Russian prisoners is vivid:

> There was rough sort of accommodation for the Russian prisoners, but buggerall food for them. There were thousands of Russians already, and they were starving. Some of them would climb over the wire and break into the bread hut at night, stuff themselves full, put bread down their coats and climb back over the wire into the camp. It didn't take their guards long to work out from their bookkeeping that more loaves of bread went in than came out the other side.

He continues:

> What the guards then did, was starve three or four Alsatian dogs, and one night when they knew the Russians were in the bread store, they threw the dogs in with them. They

> locked the door. The screaming, the yells! They wouldn't let us do anything, we couldn't do anything, all the searchlights were on us. So it was torture for us but nothing to what it would have been for the Russians. Eventually the noise died down and the guards opened the door.
>
> Out came the Russians, grinning, they had new makeshift Russian hats on, made out of the Alsatian dogs! They'd killed them. Those Russians were probably then shot, but didn't care. They ate the dogs, on the spot. They were perfect for those Russian fur hats, with the flaps turned up over their ears. It was like pleading guilty to who'd done it! They didn't care!

He concludes:

> I think that single episode demonstrated the Germans' attitude to the Russians. They called them 'unter mensch', and that's how they treated them – 'sub human'. Because Russia had not signed the Geneva Convention, the Germans were able to abuse the Russian prisoners.

×–×–×–×–×–×–×

During this period Geoff's brother Keith turned eighteen – on 18 March 1941 – making him eligible for military service. He enlisted on 7 December 1941.

8

Stalag Luft III East

In April 1942 the kriegies were taken from Barth, 350 kilometres south east to Sagan, in the depths of the Silesian dustbowl. At that time it was on the border of Germany and Poland but today, known as 'Zagan' it lies well inside Poland. They were quartered in the East Compound of Stalag Luft III at Sagan, whilst the 'escape proof' super prison 'North Compound' was being constructed. The Germans had decided that having their most troublesome airmen scattered across a number of sites was, in a multiplicity of ways, not effective. How wrong they were! At the time that North Compound commenced service, others were closed, including Luft 1 and Dulag Luft. Throughout the summer of 1942, tunnelling and other escape preparation activities progressed in East Compound. It was here that a formal committee structure was established.

Douglas Bader of *Reach for the Sky* fame, already the holder of a Distinguished Flying Cross, was a prisoner in Stalag Luft III East. Douglas had two metal prosthetic legs as a result of a flying accident when he crashed at Cranwell before the war. He was at that time serving in the permanent RAF. He had managed to rejoin the service during the war despite his physical impairment, and was shot down and captured. He was indefatigable, exuberant and never stopped harassing the guards. A German workman came to repair something in a kitchen – Douglas let down the tyres of his bicycle and stole the valves, while the others distracted the guard. The prisoners then all had to line up for three hours of phoney roll call, standing virtually to attention all that time because of what was variously seen as Bader's sense of humour, or his foolishness. The other kriegies did not see much point in provoking someone who was there to actually help them.

In between the huts of East Compound there was a brick pool – technically a fire pool – waterproofed, filled with water, which became a swimming pool in the summer. One of the keenest 'swimmers' was Bader. Someone would piggyback him out from the hut in his underpants, tin legs back in the hut, and drop him into the pool. Geoff recalls:

> Bader was a pretty good swimmer, for someone with no legs, simply dog paddling. He wanted to be in everything, but his disability inevitably made that difficult. He dearly wished to be tunnelling with the rest of the men but crawling underground was impossible.

One day Geoff learnt on the grapevine that he and Douglas were to be transferred to Colditz Castle – the supercooler for 'naughty boys'. He managed to bribe the German doctor and avoid going. Then early one morning, a group of guards and a sergeant came in, stomped through the camp, surrounded Douglas and marched him off, suspended from their shoulders. As he lurched past Geoff he called out: 'Cherub, you bastard!' He realised that Geoff had organised a bribe and was furious to have not achieved the same. 'Bye Douglas, be a good boy,' Geoff chirped. Later it was understood that Kommandant Von Lindeiner was simply not prepared to tolerate another minute of Bader's behaviour.

Geoff didn't see Douglas again until many years after the war. As a roving representative of the Shell Oil Company,

Bader visited Australia when Geoff was a respectable suburban general practitioner in Frankston, Australia, in the late 1950s. A reunion of four of the men from East Compound, was organised at the Windsor Hotel just opposite Parliament House in Melbourne. High ceilings, solid leather, terribly 'pukkah'. They had a wonderful, and boisterous night. As the organiser, Geoff went in early next morning to settle the account. The maître d'hotel looked down his nose at Geoff, remonstrating: 'Dr Cornish if you're ever considering another reunion with Captain Bader, please make it anywhere but the Windsor'.

One of the men in the hut adjacent to Geoff had attended a classy British School in the company of the Crown Prince of Denmark. The Prince regularly sent 'girlie' magazines to his friend, which were then passed around to the other kriegies. Geoff took a liking to the blonde model on the cover of one of the 'glossies'. A romantic to his bootstraps, Geoff decided to write to the magazine and ask whether he might become a penfriend to the young lady. 'Her name was Gitte; she was so beautiful!' On the magazine cover Gitte was seated on the pitched roof of a house, with her elegant legs draped either side of the chimney. 'Such lovely legs, she was a dancer,' Geoff explains. To Geoff's delight the editor wrote to say that would be acceptable, that Gitte's father was a friend of his and had given consent. No doubt this was seen as the young lady and her father's way of doing a little bit for the war effort. Geoff would correspond with Gitte for the rest of the war.

Life in the camp was punctuated by a regular bombardment of propaganda – 'Goebel's' propaganda. The daily papers were delivered by the 'paper goon', Frommel, a tiny little good-humoured peasant. He came in each day with two bundles of papers and gave them to Bill Barrett who looked after the mail. Frommel would hand over the newspapers, and the men would greet him: 'Morgen, ist Stalingrad gennomen?

'Stalingrad? Has Germany taken Stalingrad yet?' Of course they never had. After about three weeks of this he simply came in with: 'Nein, noch nicht!' They no longer asked the question.

The continental flyers were the ones who ran through the German newspapers, word by word and got a great deal of intelligence information from doing so. A picture of one of the German Aces showing a kid over a Messerschmitt fighter on the Eastern Front brought the observation:

> What the hell's he doing up in that area? He was last down in North Africa. The Germans are waiting for an attack when they move fliers of that calibre from where they have been needed and appear to have them just waiting around somewhere else.

Sure enough, reading through the death notices would reveal that 'Willy Schmidt died the hero's death' at so and so, on such and such a date. If he was last known to have been three hundred miles north of Stalingrad, the new picture would be interpreted to indicate that the Germans were expecting a counterattack near the location of the photograph. The men found uncanny, the deductions which the scrutineers drew from the available information. As predicted, in two days the counterattack would occur. Often, the intelligence had already been sent back in code to England.

René Marcinkus was an expert linguist. He taught a number of languages in the camp and supervised the analysis of all the newspapers. Of Lithuanian descent, he had grown up in Russia and travelled all over Europe as a professional soccer player before the war. He contributed substantially to the planning of escape routes and the work of the mapping department. He would later be executed following the 'Great Escape'.

Study was a useful and attractive option available to the

prisoners. Expert tuition was available in almost any subject one could think of. Courses could be undertaken through The University of London. One prisoner completed his real estate exams. A German guard tutored in the German language, presumably hoping to discover fluency or intelligence from his students. Jimmy James attended the guard's classes. Geoff was tutored in mathematics by a former Edinburgh University professor. With the number of people in the camp there was just no quiet period at all. In the evening the guards would lock the windows, bar over the wooden shutters to effect the blackout across the whole camp. They would leave the internal lights on until about 21.00 because they knew they'd have so much trouble if they didn't. It was safer to allow the men some leniency and time to themselves.

Because Geoff wanted to study:

> I went to bed very early in the bottom bunk and I got up at 3.30 or 4 in the morning as I'd done as a kid to go surfing in Perth, and I studied. I studied German, until I was absolutely word perfect in it and I knew some words of dialects as well, because I thought that, if I'm going out as a German – and fair haired, blue eyed, I could pass as a German – then I'm not going to let an Aussie accent give me away.

Because it could have meant life or death, Geoff studied German assiduously and enthusiastically. It was possible to get books easily and cheaply from the guards or from England via the Red Cross. As Geoff's fluency in the German language increased he became a part of the German Bribery Department, a subgroup of the Great Escape committee.

In late 1942, Roger Bushell arrived at East Camp, Stalag Luft III at Sagan, some 18 months after Geoff had met him in Dulag Luft.

Roger became the mastermind behind the planning of the Great Escape, and in this capacity was known by the code name 'Big X'. East Camp was where many of the escape and tunnelling techniques were devised and refined. Geoff remembers Roger clearly:

> Being a lawyer he was always after bright conversation – that was his livelihood – he couldn't ever abandon that. Even his social conversation was peppered with humour, and with educated knowledge; he could quote from Shakespeare, he could quote from Mien Kampf. He was a champion skier, a European champion downhill slalom ski champion in pre war days. He could talk on any subject and once you got him started, like any lawyer, it was tough to shut him up.
>
> Roger was generally good humoured, except when he got really mad with the Germans, when he'd say: 'bloody Huns – they say I've got to do this – well I'm not going to do it. I'm not going to do it, unless they make me!' That was his other side. He would push and resist them just as far as he could and knew their limits exactly.

Anyone who had an idea for an escape would put the proposal to a member of the escape committee, who would then put them to Roger. Next, the proposer would walk and talk with Roger and someone else from the committee. They would traipse around the perimeter pathway of the compound, so that even the prisoner's confidantes would not be able to hear the conversations. It was not that the men believed that their mates would let secrets out, but rather that if something came up inadvertently, close to where a guard was, it might be overheard. The fewer people who knew about any particular escape plan, the better.

Discussions around the perimeter with Roger were

purposeful, with Roger questioning, explaining and teasing out various options, because he knew the continent so well and had already escaped and been recaptured several times. He knew all or most of the traps and how to get out of them, and how an escapee eventually ended up back in the cooler. Any aspiring escapee had to have a contingency plan for every situation they might encounter after leaving the camp. To try and pre-empt every possible event improved one's chances of survival. Roger's German – with a slight Swiss accent – was impeccable because of the considerable time he had spent on the continent before the war.

Learning to bribe the guards was another highlight of Geoff's life in camp. The job of the bribery group, all fluent German speakers, was to procure goods and materials from the guards, to be used in espionage and in escapes. Each man had his own 'tame goon', with whom only he was allowed to converse. As Geoff became competent in the role, he gained responsibility for handling and controlling the German money, of which the prisoners held quite a large stash. Cash was the easiest exchange to effect as it was relatively plentiful, untraceable and of limited value to the guards in times when there was little to buy outside of the camp. The 'German Bribery Boys' as they were known, would trade goods from their Red Cross parcels for German money and for items from outside. The money was stored away for use by escapees, to assist them in crossing occupied territory after breaking free, when they would need to be able to pay for their food at slave labour workers' canteens.

Items which were valuable in the barter trading included coffee, chocolate – especially the dark, unsweetened 200 gram blocks, soap, and American cigarettes. Good quality coffee would come in only about one in ten parcels, and then only after America had joined in the war. American parcels were far superior to others.

When a guard was going on leave he'd be ripe for the picking. Taking home soap for his wife or chocolate for the children would ensure a first class time on his leave. That leave only came twice a year, to break his twelve hours a day, six days a week, miserable existence. The longer the war continued the wearier and more disillusioned the guards became. Those who had been more resistant to corruption in early times, were by now worn down and beginning to see the possibility that they might be on the losing side of this very long war. Those who had formerly been amenable were now dead easy. If the situations of the captors and captives might later be reversed, they were all quietly keen to increase their chances of preferential treatment.

As the bribery boys grew in confidence, they became more audacious in their requests. A guard who had previously complied with something easy and knew he had leave coming up would approach his 'briber', Geoff recalls:

> We'd say 'things are very tight, we can't give you anything' – they'd have a lousy leave. Because we'd asked them for something pretty dynamic and they'd assumed their German dignity and said 'no, I could not do that, that's impossible', we'd say 'Alright, please yourself' and close the discussion there.
>
> Then I'd say 'I'm studying physics and I need a compass needle'. The guard would know all the time why I needed it. He'd go and buy the needle and smuggle it in, trembling with fear. The next time he'd say 'I'm going on leave on Saturday' and wait for me to produce soap for his wife, chocolate for the kids and 'pure gold' – coffee. I'd say I couldn't get anything: 'things are pretty tight'.

Finally something red hot:

> 'Well I might be able to get one if you got me a radio valve'.
>
> He said he couldn't. 'Well if you don't, I'll show them the receipts from last time, from the magnet'. 'You can't prove it.'
>
> 'Yes I can.'

Another guard in our pay lived in the same town. We had said to the latter:

> 'Go into so and so's hardware store and buy a magnet, throw it in the river if you like but give us the receipt.
>
> So when the guard challenged our ability to produce a receipt, 'Bush' Parker, our Queenslander magician, would whisk it out of thin air, let the guard see it clearly, then have it disappear again.
>
> He'd be ashen! From then on he would get what was required.

Al Hake, an Australian, was expert at manufacturing compasses from old razor blades. He would cut them into slivers, held in a vice made from a window hinge, and pass them to his helpers who would pass a magnet across each one for a full day, eventually magnetising it sufficiently to enable its use as a compass needle. The compasses were an essential provision for escapers.

Sydney Dowse was assigned to Corporal Hesse who was a censor and interpreter in the Vorlager – the administration area of the complex. Dowse, who had already made several brief escapes, did not even need to speak German to do business with Hesse. Hesse passed a wide variety of documents to him, which were used for copying and forging. The Hundfürher, in charge of the security guards' dogs, did likewise. Others supplied paper, pen nibs, card and chemicals which were used to produce waterproof ink.

Geoff Hill who was in charge of the bribery department,

reported one guard to Roger Bushell who then reported him to 'Jimmy Higgins' – their nickname for the Hauptman. 'Jimmy' was a very senior man in the camp, responsible for security across the whole of East Compound. Jimmy was the same rank as most of the men – a flight lieutenant – long and deeply in the kriegies' pay. 'Jimmy' Roger confided, 'Schmidt's going to come and confess, he thinks he's only going to get a week's bread and water'.

The guard then received six weeks and a lowering in rank. He became just vicious with the system. After that incident, he would approach his contact with 'what do you want next?' He was heartily sick of the German Army and aware that the Allies might well win the war. The boys had him. They used blackmail and lies, had no scruples.

Geoff had a shock during the time in East Camp when he and another tunneller went down on the early shift. Geoff was second, was right behind the man doing the digging. The digger would push the sand back through his legs in a scoop, a refashioned *Cadbury Cocoa* tin, into the receiving container which Geoff was holding. The cocoa containers were adapted with tin snips to shape the scoops. Cans from *Klim* powdered milk, another staple from the Red Cross parcels, made little lamps which burned margarine fat, with the addition of a pyjama cord wick.

The receiving container was like a large, old fashioned greengrocer's scales, which the men had conned from one of the Russians who'd picked it from a rubbish tip. They fixed the tray onto a little wooden trolley with wooden wheels – made in the camp – and filled it with sand. When they tugged on the string the man at the other end of the tunnel would haul it back up, throw the sand into the storage bin behind him, tug the string again and the man below would pull the trolley back down.

By then the diggers would have another load ready and

over a day, a great deal of sand – up to four thousand kilograms could be removed. Two men went down the tunnel together, throwing the scoop ahead. The tunnel was squarish and a bit broader than a man's shoulders, shored on the sides and top with solid timber bed boards.

On this particular day the two men were going down the tunnel, the first on the trolley, clunkety clunk, flat on his belly as if beginning a surf. He clackety clacked his way down to the end of the tunnel and gave the customary tug on for the number two to haul it back. The number three man would still be up in the room. Geoff was waiting at the first base. All of a sudden the number one tunneller came shooting backwards on the trolley straight into Geoff:

> 'Get out of here – there's somebody down there.'
>
> Under such circumstances, when a smelly backside hits you in the face, you don't argue, Geoff acknowledges.
>
> 'Whadd'ya mean? There can't be anyone down there!'
>
> 'There's a bloody light down there, I tell you!'

Geoff remembers how difficult it was to go backwards at speed down a very narrow tunnel, 'but we got out'.

On looking back down the tunnel, the first man said 'look'!

At the end of the tunnel, they could see another lamp, just like the one they were holding. 'It took us minutes to work it out, then we realised that when we moved our lamp, the one down the tunnel moved too!'

Someone, almost without doubt Glemnitz, had found the tunnel and put a mirror at the end of it!

At that stage the tunnellers didn't have electricity. In both Luft I and East Compound they only had candles and the margarine lamps. The stinking smoke and appalling ventilation affected them badly, almost to the point of asphyxiation.

Whilst in East Compound Geoff became involved in an activity which really was his technical forté – photography. A small photographic unit was established to produce photographs for the forged documents – passports, worker's permits and myriad items being produced by the forgery unit *Dean and Dawson*, to be used by escapers. With basic equipment Geoff was able to replicate his laboratory back at the university in Perth. He knew what chemicals were needed and was able to bribe them from the guards in separate lots, then combine them himself as required, to minimise the likelihood of detection. His long-practised timing skills enabled him to judge the processing accurately and precisely.

The men were fortunate to have the services of Pieber, the 'good guard' who loaned them his Leica camera to take photographs, ostensibly to send home to their families. He would even take the film and have it developed outside of the camp, for those pictures which the kriegies judged to be sufficiently innocuous. This was necessary in order to authenticate the activity and to prevent the discovery of the photographic unit inside the camp. Geoff was assisted in the unit by Charles Hall, who had been a photographic apprentice in the RAF before the war. The two men produced an array of portraits by photographing their colleagues and by adapting the commercial products brought back into the camp by Pieber.

Although Geoff did not directly experience the following incidents, they are worthy of the telling. On one occasion two men escaped by cutting the external wire fence and running into the woods. On their recapture, Kommandant Von Lindeiner presented the men with a bottle of whiskey 'in recognition of their daring'. On another occasion, when a number of kriegies were based at Szubin, between their tenure at Barth and arrival at Sagan, they were in army care, with a particularly officious Wehrmacht colonel. After being roundly insulted by the colonel, Wings Day made a speech to his men where he reminded them of their duty to escape. Glemnitz had been equally poorly treated and was present. He told the airmen that he considered the army personnel to be *Dummköpfe* and stated that he supported the kriegies efforts to escape. Wings and Glemnitz would become good friends after the war.

9

HIGHJINKS AND HELLHOLES

The North Compound of Stalag Luft III was opened in Spring 1943. It was intended and claimed to be the perfect, escape-proof, master prison camp. It was rushed, finished quickly before its originally planned date, because the number of captives had increased exponentially once Britain's 'thousand bomber raids' were underway. The hurried construction resulted in many tasks still being incomplete when the prisoners started to move in. The moves occurred during March and early April 1943; Paul Brickhill recalls being transferred on April Fools' Day. Tunnelling began immediately.

In his 2003 book *The Great Escapers*, Historian Tim Carroll quotes an edict that was issued from High Command early in April 1943:

> Each POW has to be informed that by escaping in civilian clothing or German uniform he is not only liable to disciplinary punishment but runs the risk of being court-martialled and committed for trial on suspicion of espionage and partisanship, in the affirmative he may even be sentenced to death.

Although this attitude to the issue of disguise was inconsistent with the terms of the Geneva Convention, Von Lindeiner nevertheless ensured that the statement was promulgated. This made no difference to the kriegies determination to continue tunnelling.

The site of North Compound had not been properly cleared and vast numbers of pine trees were still to be removed. The first group of Russian labourers felled the trees and removed the parts which were required for building purposes. They left the top 'Christmas tree' pieces and the branches in piles around the grounds. Further groups of labourers would be brought on site in groups of thirty, with several guards. Each Russian would pick up a treetop and walk back to the gates. The guards would open the gates, let them out in three columns, ten to a column and they would dump the timber outside the camp perimeter for burning. After only a few weeks, Geoff and his Czech friend, Ivo Tonder hatched the idea of changing places with a couple of Russians and going out in disguise. They grew beards for a few days, smeared themselves with filth, donned Russian uniforms and hid. One Russian bent down over the trees where Geoff had hidden after roll call.

> I just threw a bar of chocolate under the next tree, motioned to him and he scuttled after it on all fours, grinned with delight and opened it up, he just – I can still see him eating that chocolate as I stood up in his place with the pine tree.

Ivo stood up with his tree and the group reassembled to go out of the gate. One of the 'machine gun' guards in the towers had seen the swap. He called out to his colleague below: 'Est ist ein Englander darunter' – 'There's an Englishman down there'. Tonder knew that as a Czech in Russian uniform, he would be shot as a spy. He just dropped his tree top there and then and sprinted. 'He was so quick, he just ran and ran, straight to the nearest open window and dived headlong through it.'

The last thing Geoff recalls clearly was the two boots disappearing. Ivo got rid of his maps, clothing and rations and the guards never found out who it had been. The guards knew it was hopeless to try and catch him; they couldn't risk leaving the columns to give chase. Geoff continues the story:

When they got to the gate, they lined us all up again – one less going out than had come in. They knew that there was a Russian in the camp but they didn't care about that. As the sentries tried to identify the stooge, the gate guard called for Pieber, *ferret extraordinaire*. Although the Russians pushed forward one of their own men, Pieber was not fooled. He quickly recognised Geoff despite his filthy disguise:

> 'Cornish kommen zie mahl mit!' 'Come with me.' He barked.
>
> 'He just picked me out and took me to the cooler, hands above my head, for 14 days bread and water.'

While that was happening, Brickhill and a party of kriegies were coming into the camp. They were made to put their hands up while this bedraggled Russian was prodded past them to the prison. They clenched their fists, calling 'Kamerid Tovarisch Joe for Koenig' – a slogan that was supposed to cheer up the 'Russian'. Paul said later:

> I have never been so surprised in my life as when this filthy Russian went past me and said in an Australian accent: 'See you in fourteen bloody days fellas!'

Geoff was duly deposited in the cooler. The guards left a book in the room. As he picked it up to read, they turned the lights out. Then they would turn the heating in the cells on full blast until he was stripped naked and perspiring, almost passing out, of course without any water to drink. Next, they would turn the heating off, open the window and let the snow in, and he'd freeze. Then they'd repeat the trick with the light and the book again. Geoff's thoughts were only on what he was going to do and how advanced things would be in the tunnel – 'which they weren't, of course, in less than 14 days. I couldn't let them get under my skin. It felt so miserable to be away from the tunnelling.'

The next morning, after his first night in the cooler, he was taken out into the courtyard for exercise. The Russian labourers came out and gave him salutes and broad grins. They were thrilled to have one of their countrymen so close. The following night there was a noise: 'I thought I heard something'.

At first light he looked around and found some fresh vegetables and an egg inside the cell door. Astonished, he stuffed them into his clothing. He tells:

I didn't ask any questions, I ate it all. The egg was a bit of a mixed blessing because you had to eat the shell as well, couldn't leave a trace of it.

I kept telling myself: 'this is good for me, I should be enjoying it.'

So the next night he waited and sure enough the door opened again. A hand came through and he could see that it belonged to one of the Russians, who was grinning widely. He left more food and disappeared. Geoff learnt later that 'they were going to look after me because I was one of them!'

This group of Russian prisoners were charged with looking after Kommandant Von Lindeiner's garden, so some of the Kommandant's best vegetables finished up under their greatcoats. They would draw lots and the successful one would break out of their compound (where they were guarded closely), wriggle along on his belly to avoid machine guns, searchlights and Alsatian dogs and into the compound where the isolation cells were. He would sneak past the guards, pick the lock on the cell door, put the vegetables in, lock the door and wriggle back. If detected he would have been killed. 'They did that the whole time I was in solitary confinement. And it was the winner who got to do that!' he relates dryly.

When Geoff's fourteen days were over and he returned to the camp, Glemnitz, who had known him from the beginning of the Stalag Luft I days, said 'Na! Ivan wie gets?' – 'How ya going, Ivan?' That became Geoff's German nickname. 'Der Schrecklich' (the terrible one).

On his return, the boys in Geoff's room had saved his rations and prepared a feast:

> I tried to eat it; I was ravenous . . . down to the toilet and threw the lot up. I had got so used to just the bread and water and the illicit vegetables, that I couldn't stomach what was to me then a rich meal.

However, he reacclimatised quickly.

Once the men were settled into the new compound Roger Bushell was appointed to the position of 'Big X', chairman of the Escape Committee. From here on the committee structures and protocols became more formalised and escaping proceeded according to several fixed principles: all escapes would be considered and decided by the committee; tunnels would be fewer and better planned; the committee would decide the location and direction of every tunnel. There were to be no more random, small tunnels or other forms of escape. It was decided that from hereon there would be only three, major tunnels. In the best British tradition they were designated *Tom, Dick and Harry*. These three tunnels were commenced from inside hut 101 and its neighbours.

The three tunnels were far more sophisticated than any before. Kriegie electricians had tapped the compound power supply and had electric lighting throughout the whole system.

A complex process of sequestering bedboards from the huts ensured that all tunnel cavities were well lined and supported although this meant that beds eventually became highly unstable – on one occasion Geoff recalls the top bunk occupant falling down onto the middle kriegie and the pair then crashing through to the man on the lowest. Air vents were spaced as well as possible through the network. The tunnellers shifts and their comings and goings were planned with precision. At all times every tunneller must have alibis above ground, and be able to appear for appell – roll call – at short notice. Feigned illness was common and tunnellers would be 'covered' by their mates above running from one hut to another and sometimes being sprung, in an effort to appear in more than one simultaneous parade.

In North Compound, given the climate of sophisticated escape planning, Geoff soon recommenced his photographic activities. Over a time the reproductions became near-perfect. Early on, the men in North Compound had made a radio to receive the BBC news at night with help from Pieber who supplied many of the required components.

A couple of unpleasant incidents occurred in the evenings, after the evening meal when the men were walking between the huts – several men were shot at when they'd tried to stray off the path. They were only injured or near-missed, but the incidents could have been fatal:

> We asked that the paths be marked out quite clearly so that we could stick to them. Fair enough, if we tried to stray away after that we were running the risk of being shot.

The Germans really had no resources to apply to altering the paths. They decided that the only way to mark it out clearly and cheaply (an idea subtly 'drip fed' to them by their charges) was to dig down to the yellow sand about two feet under the surface, and use this to mark out visible paths. Their prisoners further suggested that the Russian labourers could lay out the yellow paths. After that, the prisoners would be able to see where they were walking at night.

The next step was for the prisoners to raise the yellow paths and simultaneously raise the garden beds to the same level. The change was subtle and went unnoticed. It provided an easy means of disposal of sand from tunnelling for quite some time. Eventually, when the quantities became too much, other methods were required.

Until now the debris had been taken out of the tunnels by the disposers suspending small bags of sand around their necks. In cold weather these were easily disguised under the men's clothing but as summer approached a means was required which would not require the wearing of hot, heavy clothing.

'Penguin trousers' were invented. These were expanded long johns, worn under one's outer pants, secured tightly around the ankle so they functioned as a sort of bag and again were suspended from the wearers' shoulders. The distribution of the sand right around the wearer's legs cleverly disguised just how much sand was actually concealed. They acquired the name penguin because they caused the wearer to 'waddle'. The wearer would demonstrate his walking to his fellows to ensure that the disguise was effective. He would then wear the special trousers, filled with their booty, as he walked outside. On reaching an appropriate part of a path or garden bed he would loosen the bottoms of the pants and allow the sand to trickle out. They got rid of a lot of sand that way.

On one occasion the men were not quite quick enough and Glemnitz noticed yellow sand on the garden beds before it had been properly mixed in with the grey topsoil. He ordered the ferrets to do a search and they donned their boiler suits and did so. The unearthing of more yellow sand seemed to satisfy the searchers and activities resumed. There was an intermittent flurry of probing the soil, crawling under huts and trench digging, but no incriminating discoveries were made. Rubberneck hid himself in a hut kitchen one afternoon and the boys locked him in. Hours later he blustered his way out, furious. They found Glemnitz, embarrassed at being caught, under the same hut.

Walking around inside the perimeter wire was a favourite form of exercise and the only safe place to conduct confidential discussions. It was about a kilometre around the perimeter wire and inside that was a warning wire rail, three metres in from the barbed wire and the tall fences, 'no man's land'. If anyone went past the warning wire, they could be shot on sight.

Again, as they had done at Barth, the Eastern Continental pilots would quiz the Russian prisoners. Later in the war, they gleaned that Russian researchers were working at Peenemunde on the Baltic coast, at the V1 and V2 rocket development sites. They were able to pinpoint exactly where they were and exactly what stage they were at, and get that intelligence back to England, by radio and by handwritten coded letters. As a result, the RAF precision bombing of Peenemunde on 17-18 August 1943 delayed that experimental programme by at least two months and lessened the severity of the eventual V2 attack. The moonlight raid on Peenemunde killed over 180 Germans and hundreds of Polish slave labourers.

Hauptman 'Jimmy Higgins' had supplied the men with various components towards the manufacture of their radios and one afternoon he furtively but anxiously gave the men a tip: 'The Gestapo are going to make a surprise search of this hut tonight. They must not find anything or I'm finished!'

Around 03.00, the tramp of heavy boots surrounded the

hut. When the Gestapo entered the Kommandant warned them to be careful. 'These kriegies are smart, they use every trick in the trade.' The officials smirked, locked one door. Every prisoner was made to file through the other doorway, beside which a small table had been placed. It was a stinking hot, humid night and the Gestapo standing on either side of the table took off their coats and hung them behind the door. Geoff describes the proceedings:

> We had to stand while we were being strip-searched, all two hundred of us in the hut. Steadily there mounted on the table, a collection of bits and pieces – scraps of paper, bits of old compasses and so on, which we'd allowed them to find. They were quite pleased with themselves by this stage.
>
> It eventually came Queenslander 'Bush Parker's' turn to be searched. He was a bushman, a professional magician and sleight of hand expert. Halfway through being searched he dropped a small compass and grabbed it up again. The Gestapo snatched his wrist: 'give it to me!'
>
> 'Bush' let them believe that he could not speak German. They prised open his fingers but nothing was there. 'Is this what you're looking for?' he said, and hauled the compass out of his hair.
>
> 'That must be seized!'
>
> He hid it again then produced it from under his arm. He pretended to be ticklish and collapsed on the floor whenever the bloke touched him. It was so good to be able to laugh at the Gestapo and get away with it!
>
> Furious, exasperated, the officer called to his colleague: 'Come and give me a hand with this man,' which his mate duly did. Finally 'Bush' let them have the compass and made his exit. The Gestapo turned around and not a prisoner was left in the whole hut. The table was clear – there was nothing left.

> The Gestapo were in possession of the whole hut with nothing in it! They were absolutely livid, put on their jackets and stormed to the exit gate. 'Let us out, take us to the Kommandant' they bellowed.
>
> They felt in their pockets and they were empty. The kriegies had pinched their passes to get out of the camp. They realised what a vulnerable position they were in.
>
> Eventually the Kommandant arrived. 'Schweinhund! Rotten sods have pinched our passes' they roared. 'Shoot them, court martial them, do what you like!'
>
> 'This camp is under excellent control,' the Kommandant responded. 'Wait while we retrieve your passes. Just a few moments.'
>
> Meantime, the forgery boys were applying an old rubber boot heel, into which had been carved a rubber stamp. Every letter which left the camp was stamped with the Swastika, the German Eagle and the word 'Geprüft' (approved). When the Kommandant came to get the passes, he smiled. He nearly burst his sides trying not to laugh. Each had the RAF Crown of England above RAF wings, and then 'Approved – Stalag Luft III.'
>
> The Gestapo Officers could see for themselves that the joke was on them.

Observers described them as 'ashen'. The Kommandant was on the side of the kriegies; by now he hated the Gestapo as much as they did. No one ever heard what happened to the inspection team.

During their time as prisoners many of the Englishmen expressed a desire to get away from England after the war was over, either to New Zealand, Australia or Canada. A lot of enquiries were addressed to the Australians' senior officer, Wing Commander Larkin. Larkin decided to form what he called a 'brains trust'. He selected eight of the Australians from different walks of life and if one of the English expressed interest in learning about a particular field in Australia he was put onto one or all of the 'brains trust'.

The brains trust included Paul Brickhill who had been a Sydney journalist before the war and could speak about Sydney, journalism and related careers. Paul would later write a popular book, the tale of the prisoners' exploits, 'The Great Escape'. Rod Ferry had been a farmer, so he possessed expertise about life on the land and what to expect there. Larkin himself was a career air force officer so he could speak about what it had been like in the services pre-war and what it might be like after the war. Geoff was included because he had worked at a university, was conversant with university ways, and had started his degree before applying to join the RAF. 'I had a pretty fair idea of what university life was like, what costs were like, although I didn't know how the universities in other states compared.'

The 'Australian Brains Trust' would assist their fellows to transform their vague thoughts or dreams into action plans for the future. Geoff was so moved by this opportunity to market his beloved Australia that he decided to take action of his own:

> I can remember writing a letter, a very treasured letter when we were only allowed three a month. I wrote to the Western Australian Agent General in London saying that many of the men were wanting to migrate to Australia, and I felt that Western Australia was the state 'that's got a lot to offer them'. I also stated that they were very well educated, many at tertiary level, were mature and were saving money, because our air force pay was accruing in a bank account. 'We should be able to do something special to attract them to come to the West'.

Geoff mailed off his letter. Shortly after, one morning when his father opened the *West Australian*, on the front page was his son's letter from Germany, printed in full! Fred was delighted and proud.

10

One escape after another

Notwithstanding the gratification Geoff derived from tunnelling, bribery and photography, by far the highlight of his time in the POW camps was learning the rudiments of medical practice. After achieving competence in the German language, Geoff turned to revising his science education and applying it to the field of medicine, to the study of which he had so long aspired.

Medical and in fact any textbooks could be bought for a song – or a couple of cigarettes. No one in the German villages had the slightest interest in studying because everyone of university age was one way or another engaged in war. Those left behind – mothers and children – had far more immediate concerns.

Geoff acquired some old German textbooks and set to work. As usual his ritual was to rise very early and study until breakfast and tunnelling time. His big thrill was when Dr Monteuuis, the British kriegie doctor did his 'rounds'. Monteuuis came in while appell was being held, would make his way through all fifteen huts and check the men who were too sick to attend. The usual complaints were diarrhoea, pneumonia or unhealed wounds. The doctor would inspect and minister to his patients, then go and give Geoff a tutorial to supplement the material that he was studying from the German textbooks.

Dr Monteuuis – whom the boys soon came to know as 'Twee' – couldn't speak a word of German. He belonged to that class of Englishmen who thought that 'if one speaks English slowly enough and loudly enough the stupid bastards will understand one'. He joked about his Spanish ancestry, saying that his progenitors had reached Britain in the Armada, when many galleons were wrecked off the Irish coast and the men on board were captured. They had been taken in by the locals, slept with the women and conquered peacefully. Monteuuis had graduated from Middlesex hospital only a couple of years before being captured at Dunkirk.

The Germans had their own doctor, Major 'Stabsarzt' Hildebrandt. He was responsible for all the soldiers in the field and for the guards. The welfare of the prisoners came under his supervision. He was based at the Luftwaffe base some ten kilometres away, a developmental and experimental base where aircraft and other military products were tested. Hildebrandt would come down and inspect the hospital and Geoff would act as his interpreter, so that he could communicate with Dr Monteuuis and with their patients. Geoff learnt a great deal from his listening and interpreting. The men considered Hildebrandt to be a doctor first, a gentleman second and an enemy third. After the war Geoff tried to track him down but was unsuccessful. The last the kriegies saw of him was when they were separated during the Russian advance.

During their post-appell tutorials Geoff would take the opportunity to learn all he could.

> 'What difficulties are you having?' Monteuuis would ask.
>
> 'I couldn't understand this or that,' Geoff would reply, 'and then he'd tell me about it.'
>
> 'It was wonderful, we had a lovely rapport. It took me away from what was going on around me,' he still enthuses today.

After a time, Geoff was assigned as a helper in the camp lazarett (hospital). Dr Monteuuis had an enthusiastic apprentice and Geoff gained a tutor whom he considered to be without peer. He relates:

> Doctor Monteuuis showed me what to do, why we were doing it and how often we had to do it, and then supervised me. We had eight beds in the hospital and we did a ward round every morning and every afternoon.

The patients were curious, both about their treatment and about the role of Dr Monteuuis' 'shadow': 'What the hell are you doing there doc?' the men would ask.

Monteuuis would explain what he was doing and why. Geoff considers that this example of professionalism and humanity prior to doing his own medical training, influenced his medical practice for life. Seeing what would now be called 'hands on' medicine in such a dramatic set of life circumstances stayed with him, as did the horrific scenes which he was later to witness. 'I learnt then to always explain to patients what I am doing, why I am doing it and what the outcome is most likely to be.'

Geoff tells us:

> Medical supplies from the Germans were quite limited. One remedy was *fisch salbe* – a sort of fish ointment, very good for drawing boils and as a primitive antiseptic. It was applied to most skin conditions. There were no antibiotics then, and it was during that time that the Germans developed the first of the sulphonamides. The first aspirin was available, having been invented by Bayer during the First World War. Pneumonia was one of the main chest complaints but the Germans' primitive antibacterial sulphanilamide was a wonderful antidote to

that. Sulphaguanidine was good too, it stayed in the bowel where the organism was fighting the infection.

x–x–x–x–x–x–x

About midway through his time in North Compound, Geoff learned of his brother's death. Keith had joined the RAAF when he turned eighteen in December 1941 and was killed when his Beaufort aircraft failed on takeoff in New Guinea on 16 October 1943. It was Keith's first operational flight; the plane had a full bombload and exploded on impact. The Beaufort aircraft were notorious for mechanical failure.

Dot Cornish could not believe what had happened. She could not reconcile the values of Christianity, a fair and just God, with what had happened to her family. Two sons shattered by war. One in prison all this time and now the second, dead. Dot never recovered from the tragedy.

x–x–x–x–x–x–x

One day in early January 1944, Dr Monteuuis approached Geoff:

> Geoff, these tutorials are going to have to stop, unfortunately. I'm sorry, but this camp is full to brimming and they've opened another at Belaria, about three kilometres away. It's an old Luftwaffe barracks and they're posting me to it because there are five or six doctors here and none there.
>
> I want you to come with me as my interpreter and assistant and I'll push medicine into you, morning noon and night.

Geoff thought long and hard. The choice between escaping

through the tunnel or learning more about medicine, was stark. He elaborates upon his quandary:

> My escape 'persona' was a Danish milk specialist. My hometown was nineteen railway stations from Copenhagen. My mother was a nurse and my father a schoolmaster. I could recite the name of every station, in order. We also learnt the names of the hangouts where German soldiers on leave would go. All the dancehalls, pubs and cinemas.
>
> If I were caught the Gestapo would bring in a Danish quisling to interrogate me, so I had to be detail perfect. My mission was to go to Freiberg to investigate an outbreak of a cattle disease. I had been briefed on every aspect of the terrain and layout by those who had been there.
>
> Eventually I went in and told the Escape Committee what I wanted to do, that I wanted to go with Dr Monteuuis.

Roger Bushell objected:

> 'You can't go!'
>
> 'Why not?'
>
> 'Unless you can get someone else to take the photographs for the forged passports and escapees' documents. The only way I'll let you go is if you find a replacement for the photo work.'

Geoff went away to think again. Before he returned:

> I decided to ask Charles Hall who was working with me. Although his skill had originally been in taking photographs, he had helped with the processing side for a long time by now. I really wanted to go with Dr Monteuuis.
>
> After explaining my predicament I asked him directly:

> 'Charles do you want to go out in the escape, through the tunnel? I can give you my position, number eight, if you'll take over my photo work.'
>
> 'You're bloody mad!' he replied in disbelief.

Geoff reiterated why he was asking, why he wanted to change his plans and what Charles's added duties would be. 'I've thought about it, I'm going with "Twee".' Charles agreed, seriously wondering about Geoff's sanity.

Sixty years later Geoff clearly remembers his reasoning:

> I had two choices . . . I'd distilled them out carefully, selfishly, for my own good. If I ever did get out and went back to England and became a doctor I could not have held my head up because I had turned my back on my own doctor. He wanted me to help with our mates, he couldn't have coped with the numbers on his own.

So Geoff moved to the new, Belaria lazarett with Dr Monteuuis and settled into a routine of thinking medicine day and night. Ultimately the two were again unable to manage the number of sick men, and 'Pop' Coventry arrived. 'Pop' was so named because he had attained the advanced age of thirty! He was from Liverpool and had done a year's medical studies before the war. He'd been shot down just near Belaria when the camp first opened. At first he would come around to talk, to be in a medical environment, to fill in time. Then he joined in the tutorials, and Twee invited him to move into their room as the third man in the medical team.

Geoff describes their experience:

> Monteuuis and his two assistants and interpreter, we had a wonderful time. We had an excellent partnership. We worked

> hard, and he pushed medicine into us dramatically. One day Pop was making a bed and had his finger pierced and poisoned by the steel needle of a glass syringe, which had been left behind from testing reflexes. It had been put down, point up and forgotten. Pop had severe blood poisoning, we thought he was going to die. The finger became infected and had to be amputated. We joked about what a good gynaecologist he could be!

While Pop was out of action, which was quite a while, the medicos found another recruit for their group. Eric Stephenson had also done the first year of a medical course in England before the war, thrown in his studies to join the RAF and gone into air crew. He was shot down in September 1943 and joined Pop and Geoff at Belaria in January 1944 when he lumbered in, wearing a plaster cast on his right leg.

While the men were concentrating on their medical activities in Belaria, escape activity and planning continued in North Compound. Overnight on 24–25 March, seventy six escapers were to finally make their breakout. The date was finally determined because 'Rubberneck' was going on leave and the men wished to make good their escape during his absence. However Rubberneck unwittingly had the last word on logistics. He organised the removal of nineteen of the most significant kriegies to Belaria, a matter of days before he went on leave.

The two hundred men hoping to exit the tunnel made their way towards and into 'Harry'. Hours later and after many delays, when the first few broke through they found that their tunnel exit was some ten metres short of the woods. They were now to exit the opening in full glare of camp floodlights, within sight of the guards, not in the safety of the woods. The escape attempt continued and a stream of men, at a much slower rate than planned, made their way out and headed for the woods. By the time they were spotted, seventy six were outside and a long queue was waiting in the tunnel. Australian Bill Fordyce was one who had to turn around inside the tunnel and return whence he had come.

Hitler was outraged and declared that all recaptured men were to be executed. His advisers, led by Goering, argued with him at length. Eventually, under the pressure, he reduced the scope of the directive so it would apply only to the first fifty men recaptured.

Over several days seventeen escapers were returned to Sagan, four more sent to Saschenhausen, two to Colditz and fifty were 'shot while trying to escape'. The fifty were in fact all shot from behind while being allowed to relieve themselves on the roadside at the invitation of their custodians. When Colonel Massey, the Senior British Officer in North Compound was informed that forty-one escaping officers had been 'shot whilst trying to escape' he asked 'how many were wounded?' The reply was 'None, and I am not permitted to give you any further information, except that their bodies and personal effects will be returned to you.'

All were horrified, prisoners and Luftwaffe officers alike. Hauptman Pieber said to Massey, 'You must not think the Luftwaffe had anything to do with this . . . we do not wish to be associated . . . it is terrible.' The list of forty seven names was posted up in the camp and an update later added three more.

Prisoners were informed of the tragedy in much the same manner across all locations although they knew informally from their minders well before the announcement was made. They knew word perfectly the details of Massey's questions and answers. Geoff's words are: 'They just came out and told us. We were devastated.'

Charles Hall, Geoff's replacement in the breakout was one of the fifty who were executed. He had been an only son. Geoff was devastated and sixty years' on, he still anguishes:

> I squibbed that job of going back and seeing his parents. What would I say? What could I say? What could I do? 'I'm glad that I took the decision I did and your son was shot and I wasn't' or 'I'm sorry that he was shot and I wasn't'?

The ghost lingered long.

> I wasn't sorry. I couldn't say I was sorry – I wasn't. We were all fatalists. Charles would have seen it the same way.

x–x–x–x–x–x–x

The prisoners always regarded themselves as still being in service and on duty. They tried to keep as many Germans as possible busy, because every single one engaged with the prisoners was one less at the front. They were the orders. If anyone did escape and couldn't get any further they were to stay put and organise the local resistance – harass the Gestapo with every device and bit of energy that they had. This principle no doubt exacerbated the fuss which the Germans made about the men who had successfully broken out of Stalag Luft III on that evening in March, 1944. When they realised that so many skilled, well educated, fit, highly motivated leaders of resistance were suddenly loose, they were enraged. Had the escapees survived, they might well have caused the Fuehrer and his regime considerable grief. Tim Carroll, in a recent television interview, estimates that the Great Escape effort may have diverted 500,000 Germans from their primary focus of war, if one accounted for the role of civilians as well as the military.

x–x–x–x–x–x–x

Shortly after the escape from Stalag Luft III the British made their biggest onslaught against Nuremberg. On 30 March 1944, 782 RAF bombers took flight to pass over Nuremberg in a 68 mile stream over 17 minutes, to concentrate the destruction of the raid. Although the evening's activity destroyed 90 percent of the city, 96 bombers failed to return and 545 airmen were killed, more than had died in the entire Battle of Britain. Again the visual exposure suffered by the invaders in the bright moonlight precipitated their doom.

All this time the kriegies were well informed of the increasing success of the allies because their secret radios were working overtime. From the BBC and other sources, they knew that the tide was turning and superiority, especially in the air, was being reversed. They knew that big things were afoot before D Day and were jubilant but unsurprised at the news of the Normandy landings.

They took every opportunity to sap the morale of the guards – in fact made every opportunity that they could – and revelled in not so subtly 'rubbing their noses in it'.

x–x–x–x–x–x–x

By the end of 1944 Geoff had learnt a great deal from Dr Monteuuis.

11

Everybody out

As 1945 began it became clearer to both the prisoners and their minders that the climate of war was heating up. News trickled through that things were changing on the Eastern Front and on Wednesday 17 January, German radio announced that Russian forces were approaching the camps and that progressively, all compounds of Stalag Luft III were to be evacuated. An influx of Red Cross parcels was received and at last the men were put back on a reasonable diet. Rumour had already long indicated that camps in the East had been abandoned. The men were becoming quite excited. Refugees were sometimes seen passing outside the camp and German ME-262 jet fighters were regularly seen overhead. The men tried to go about their usual daily business but tension continued to mount.

On Thursday 25 January the Russian troops reached Steinau on the Oder River, less than 90 km east of Sagan. On Saturday evening 27 January, the men were rehearsing, aptly, *The Wind and the Rain* in North Compound and watching *You Can't Take It With You* in South, when Colonel Goodrich entered the latter theatre and announced that orders from Berlin gave the men thirty minutes to leave the camp.

Geoff was still in the Belaria compound assisting Dr Monteuuis, along with Pop Coventry and Eric Stephenson. Some five hundred ill and injured men were there. His recollection is that the Germans were ready to run: 'planmessig verkurzungen der linien' . . . 'a preplanned shortening of our forward lines'. The guards shouted orders: 'everybody out in half an hour! Jedermann raus!'

'Snowing like hell! You had to put everything that you wanted for the rest of your life, on your back, and head off into the snow.' The snow was six inches deep and still falling when the marchers commenced their journey. Off they went, just marching westward. From 23.00 hours Saturday, right through until late in the evening of Sunday 28 January 1945, successive groups left Sagan to march, they knew not where. Although the snow made marching difficult and slowed their departure, it enabled the men to load some of their belongings onto makeshift sleds which they had fashioned from benches and tables.

The men of South Compound were the first to go and had the most pressure and the most unpleasant time. By 6.00 am, over a period of seven hours, West, North, Centre and East Compounds had all been vacated. The Belaria occupants did not evacuate until late on Sunday evening. Dr Monteuuis approached Geoff: 'I'm leaving you in charge of the Lazarett. You speak German, some Russian and a bit of Polish. You know the diagnoses and you know the treatments.' Geoff had learnt his Russian and Polish from the Polish prisoners.

So Geoff and Pop stayed behind and tended to the injured and ill and Monteuuis and Stephenson moved forward with the columns of forced marchers. Others' accounts of this time indicate that those remaining managed quite well as there were mountains of provisions left behind, including tens of thousands of cigarettes and many Red Cross parcels.

Eventually those remaining – Geoff, Pop, other staff and the men – would also have to leave. On 6 February, the guards conjured up some 'stinking cattle trucks' – a bunch of old boxcars in which they were to be transported. Those too ill to travel were taken back to the hospital at North Compound; everyone else was packed into the trucks and sent off into the night. Geoff and Pop gathered what medical supplies they could and went with the cattle trucks. 'Some of the stretchers were stacked three deep with feeble bodies,' Geoff recalls. Every time the train stopped, Geoff and Pop would go along and see what they could do. They were the doctors now.

The troops had already marched well ahead and it was clear that the Russians would soon take the hospital and the now-empty compounds. The men heard gunfire during the day and saw flashes of anti-aircraft fire and artillery by night. The captured airmen later learned that Goering wanted all airmen safeguarded, as his bartering chip in the event of an allied victory. The stakes grew higher. As the Russians came really close, the Germans became even more desperate to keep hold of their human booty.

x–x–x–x–x–x–x

The diary of Michael Horsfall, a British fighter pilot based in Belgium, shows that at 12.30 hours on 14 January he had embarked upon a photographic reconnaissance sortie over Düsseldorf. A dogfight above Hinsich led to his being chased and shot down. He baled out of his burning Spitfire XI and was captured by the Gestapo at 14.30 hours. He was taken to SS headquarters after dark then to solitary confinement at Enschede . Michael continued to keep his accurate diary, on a tiny, well hidden single sheet of paper.

In hospital the next day he found the local people friendly. He describes a 'vile encounter' on the way where he was called 'terrorflieger' and 'schweinhund'. Over the next few days he was degradingly strip searched, photographed, fingerprinted and repeatedly interrogated. By 26 January they heard 'First news of big Russian break-through!' Civilians began asking the kriegies about their attitude towards Russia. 'Goons worried' his diary records. On 28 January he was moved to Dulag Luft and then to Wetzlar. On 30 January 1945, Michael departed by train for Nuremberg which he reached on 1 February. At 1230 hours he was placed in Stalag XIIID. His diary records:

> Put through de-louser. Highly undignified. Lagered 1730. No food and bloody awful conditions. Two taps for 400–500. Block 4. Under Wehrmacht.

X–X–X–X–X–X–X

The first marchers from Sagan also reached Nuremberg on 1 February, 1945, three days and nights after their departure. They were initially placed in Stalag XIIID and also put through delousing. The delousing process entailed each man placing all of his possessions and clothing, (except cooking utensils) into a sheet and rolling it up to be steamed. The men themselves went through showers.

After the Luft III men, who included many Americans, arrived on 8 February, everyone was transferred to Stalag VI. On 10 February, Geoff's group arrived by train – now only about 200 RAF airmen, who had either been sick or newly shot down, who were placed with the nearly 1500 Americans in the camp. Mike's diary records that they 'formed a British Block under Rusty Wardell; Bill Fluck adjutant'. It would have been here that he and Geoff first met. Michael's diary details RAF Mosquito raids on 14 and 15 February and large United States Army Air Force – USAAF – raids on 20 and 21 February. A Mustang was seen to cross the camp 'losing glycol' – engine coolant – on 23 February and a night raid landed a bomb only 500 yards away from the perimeter on the night of 26 February. On 27 February a Red Cross parcel issue occurred and the men had a shower! On 3 March it snowed. On 13 March the Protecting Power made a visit to the camp followed by more Red Cross parcels on 14 March. Horsfall's diary states that on 17 March there were 'Very impressive RAF night raids; Goons drop decoy flares'; and 'Incessant flieger alarm over this period'. 21 March was the 'first night without alert'.

Conditions in every location to which the prisoners had been sent, were equally appalling. The camps were overcrowded and more and more occupants flooded in daily. Garbage and sanitation were grossly inadequate and epidemics became commonplace again. The men's depleted physical condition meant they had little resistance and succumbed to every infection. Before parcels arrived, the men were already very malnourished and wasting. Retired Colonel Pellet, the last Commanding Officer of 'Stalag XIII D Nuremberg-Langwasser' whose official report is posted on the Internet, claims that 6000 US and British crew members had been moved in. 'Nuremberg-Langwasser' was the name of a creek used to identify the then undeveloped area, and is today the name of the suburb.

Historian Arthur Durand, in *Stalag Luft III: the Secret Story*, recounts that the prisoners at Nuremberg lodged a complaint with the Protecting Power on 13 March 1945. It listed nutrition and sanitation deficiencies including a calorie intake below 1300 per day; the presence of worms in their vegetables; overcrowding and lack of heating which caused increased disease and the quarters being overrun with fleas, lice, bedbugs, and rats. The complaint further pointed out the breach of the Geneva Convention constituted by locating the prisoners within three kilometres of a military target. The railway marshalling yards and the camp were side by side. Although at this time no bombs had landed within the camp, the yards themselves had been accurately bombed on a daily basis. 'During the three weeks before the submission of the report, the target had been bombed repeatedly, and many bombs had fallen near the camp,' the complaint read.

The site of Stalag XIII for the Dulag 'Durchgangslager–transit' camp had originally been because of its proximity to these Nuremberg rail marshalling yards, which were strategically critical to the movement of captives and troops. It was at all times a prime target. Stalag XIII, originally a Nazi stormtroopers camp had, prior to 1945 been a prison camp for enemy civilians of many nationalities. British and American captives were brought there later in the war, when the Sagan compounds were hurriedly evacuated in the face of the Russian advance. At its peak in 1940, the Nuremberg camp had housed over 150,000 men in barracks designed for 200. Durand explains that: 'Soviet soldiers, enlisted men and officers, had to stay in Nuremberg, assigned to work here [because] the USSR had not signed the Geneva Convention – but not before April 1943 when an official Stalag had been re-established here – Stalag XIIID'. This meant that although it was a contravention to place the citizens of signatory nations here, [in substandard conditions] there was nothing to prevent the location being chosen to house the non-signatory Russians [*unter mensch*].

Colonel Pellet's report on the world wide web further explains that in August 1943, Stalag XIIID had been damaged heavily by an allied air raid. Two thirds of the wooden barracks were destroyed by fire but only two Soviet soldiers were identified as casualties of the attack. He describes frequent bombing of Nuremberg and 'merely symbolic sheltering facilities' for the densely concentrated population within the barbed wire fences.

Although Pellet reports no other attack specifically against the camp itself, he states that many POWs were injured or killed in the city area, most of them Soviets but some Americans as well. The rail marshalling yards were bombed by the RAF by night and the Americans by day. Canadian kriegie George Sweanor in his 1979 interview with Arthur Durand described the raids as 'horrible and fascinating'. A constant wailing of air raid sirens would be heard in the distance and when the sound became intense George and the others would open the windows of the huts, to reduce the impact of the shattering glass inside. In similar fashion to Geoff's experience of bombings while he was training in England, the raiding aircraft could be identified by sound. In Sweanor's words to Durand:

> The drone of high-flying Merlin engines became perceptible and, as the throb grew inexorably in volume, it seemed to chant: 'You've had it, chum, here we come, rumm rumm; you've had it, chum, here we come, rumm rumm.' With the Lancasters and Halifaxes, however, it was like watching a play . . . the fast and usually single Mosquito aircraft, were short and sharp . . . the sharp cracks of hundreds of flak guns ushered in the next act with ear-splitting din; then red and green marker flares cascaded from the depths of the night sky.

Those below said 'somebody's going to get it', saw the smoke marker come out from the leading aircraft, and realised: 'God, we're the target!' They watched them coming, and tried to count the B-52 Super Fortresses, the heavy bombers and the fighters. Again, Sweanor recalled: 'There was no doubt now as to the target for tonight. I watched, fascinated, as the brilliant markers seemed to be drifting straight for my open mouth'. His eyes remained glued to the scene. Suddenly, 'Two walls of flame erupted in front of us as the sound of exploding bombs deafened us; I could feel the heat on my face'.

Geoff and his mates found that the Germans would not allow any of the prisoners who had been aircrew, to go down into the slit trenches. They said 'you dished this stuff out, you sit on top'. Having experienced the bombing of Coventry, Geoff still vows he would rather live through that twenty times than once this bombing of the outskirts of Nuremberg.

Others' experience was that the bombs were close, and although there were slit trenches, the guards were under instruction to shoot anyone who ventured outside the huts. Eventually many prisoners disregarded the orders, leapt through the windows and dived into the trenches. The guards were too busy looking after themselves to fire a single shot. Sweanor's memoir – *It's all pensionable time* – records:

> The scene before us was one that had to be seen to be believed. It was a most beautiful maze of light and colour that hid the stench of death. Powerful blue and white searchlights made an ever changing lattice of colours, and died . . . a particularly large blossom would go streaking downwards followed by an orange trail of light as another bomber and crew were written off. At the base . . . were countless tongues of flames, growing in size and number; their dance pausing frequently to merge with dull red glows as two-ton bombs exploded.

Nevertheless, Geoff states, not a single bomb landed in the camp. As the men saw American bombers fall, on fire, it brought back to every one, the memory of their own descents. They counted the parachutes as they came out of the burning planes: 'One, two, oh, come on – more, four and schusshhing.' One which had a wing blown off, drifted like a falling leaf.

When the German fighters came screaming down, the occupants could not believe their luck when they didn't crash in the camp. One of them almost did, a night fighter in flames – Geoff recalls him appearing determined to go straight through the men's hut, but missing them by a whisker. The plane exploded only a few hundred yards away.

Sweanor remembers:

> The tortured metal of a blazing Lancaster screamed overhead, barely missing our hut, and, escaping its tormentors, plunged to its death in the trees just outside the wire. We were all several shades whiter.

He continues:

> Most of us had escaped from aircraft in similar death plunges. The formidable raid lasted less than an hour but 'seemed an eternity'. As the last bombers turned for home to bacon and eggs and soft beds, ugly black smoke, welling up from the fires of Nuremberg, blotted out the stars.

X–X–X–X–X–X–X

12

The forced march

Michael Horsfall records that on 25 March 1945 'ten trucks of parcels arrive' and that British operations commenced east of the Rhine. Durand explains that trucks began crossing the border from Switzerland on 6 March, following an agreement reached on 24 February in Geneva. Until the trucks began arriving the prisoners had no idea that any help was imminent.

Michael's diary next says it is 'grand weather . . . [with] masses of gunfire in the distance'. On the next day he characteristically understates his view of the American Forces: 'Sammy comes into his own'.

On 28 March Michael records a 'flap caused by threatened evacuation of Wurzburg' and reveals his still balanced outlook with: 'saw mallards mating; grass growing green; bashed my birthday cake'. On 1 April: 'two formations of Thunderbolts are overhead and reports come through of the Seventh [Russian] Army reaching Wurzburg. On 2 April:'a squadron of P-38s overhead' and on 3 April, there is a 'grand flap over move'.

In the last week of March 1945, Patton's men crossed the Rhine, reportedly against orders. Geoff says that:

> He had been told to stop at the Rhine, but went straight for Nuremberg,'Blood and guts' was the way he fought. A classic wartime crossing, of building one's own bridges to get tanks

across. It is seen as one of the first and best examples of good old 'American know-how'.

The worm had turned.

×–×–×–×–×–×–×

Meanwhile, in the camp, the guards again said 'Jedermann raus!' Off the prisoners went. They departed Nuremberg on 4 April, to march to Moosburg. This was almost two months after their arrival at Nuremburg.

Nearly ten thousand men commenced the 'forced march' including the former Stalag Luft III prisoners and the remaining Americans. They covered 25 kilometres on the first day, which took them to Pöling where they slept in barns.

Article Seven of the Geneva Convention specifies that prisoners of war are not to march more than 20 kilometres a day whereas it is recorded that the South Compound men marched 34.5 miles (over 50 kilometres) in the first twenty four hours. Two or three men were reported killed at the back of the column and American fighters were overhead all day, bombing and strafing – these fighters killed a number of their own countrymen. The trip by foot took between eight and ten hours, depending where one was in the column.

On 5 April Michael notes that it is his birthday, although his cake had been eaten days before, and that by 10.00 am the marchers had reached Neumarkt. Both Michael's and second lieutenant George Wenthe's diaries relate the heavy air raid on Nuremberg. George Wenthe, a Canadian kriegie whose *Daily Log, April 4–June 4, 1945* is reproduced by Durand, states: 'later heard 147 American kriegies killed, 2000 Russ-Serbs [sic], and 40 goons'. Another report states that on this day a column of American officers at the periphery of Nuremberg was hit, with 29 men killed, during a United States Army Air Force raid.

X–X–X–X–X–X–X

Michael's diary has been invaluable in enabling Geoff's memories of this time to be placed in an accurate context, because the latter's intensive involvement with the marchers' medical condition over the coming weeks meant that he seldom even knew through what territory he was passing.

Pop Coventry and Geoff banded up together. On the first night they carried one blanket with them, as well as their foodstuffs and all the medical supplies for the column. At night they went along and patched up the men as best they could. The marchers' lives depended on them – if a kriegie couldn't walk they could be shot by the SS. The SS were about a day behind the column.

When the prisoners had all been tended, the guards would come in to see 'Herr Doktor' as they did not have a doctor of their own. Geoff was the same rank as their own captain. After only a few hours along the route the American B-51s appeared overhead, shooting at the column. A number of men were wounded and required to be moved out to a French hospital. To try to prevent further destruction, the marchers went into a farmhouse, 'liberated' a couple of white sheets and tore them into strips. When the next wave of fighters came over they displayed the word 'POW ' in twenty foot high letters at the back of the column. The fighters pulled up, came back again, turned, and recognised the American uniforms. From then the fighters became their guardian angels. The USAAF sent out a patrol at night (to bed the marchers down), another in the morning when they started to move, and a midday sortie to see how they were progressing. They circled around to see exactly where they were and sometimes waggled their wings.

This enabled Geoff to say to the guard in charge:

> No funny business, no indiscriminate shooting! You are losing the war; you can see that! Now, I can guarantee you a job after the war in Australia.'

The guard's eyes opened wide.

> You play square by me. I'm from Western Australia. I've got a fair amount of influence there. I can get you a job as Chief Lighthouse Keeper at Kalgoorlie. My grandfather was an important man there!

Geoff emphasised that it was a very responsible job because it was quite a way in from the coast, not elaborating that it was a full four hundred miles! 'The guard was so grateful. On the first night he really wanted to impress.'

At the end of the first day Geoff pointed to one of the nicest looking dwellings in the village:

> 'I want that house,' he commanded the guard.
>
> 'But that's the mayor's house,' was the reply.
>
> 'So?' Geoff asserted.

He tells us:

> The guard went into the house and ordered the occupants to leave. Do you reckon he was ropeable? They all just packed out of the house and it became the sick quarters for the night!

By nightfall on 5 April, the men had reached the town of

Berching. Michael had 'drawn half a loaf' (in a ballot for food) and was 'billeted in a church'. Wenthe's diary reports:

> Up early and cooked breakfast. Civilians very hospitable. A small boy showed us American and British flags he had ready for use soon. All think the war soon over. Had first goon issue [of] brot soup at 1 pm . . . kriegies starting to straggle, also goons. Start of complete disorder of march. Rained all the way . . . was bedded in a Catholic church. Slept near altar. Very tired feet and wounded leg.

On 6 April , George Wenthe's diary says that he ate his first egg for a year, and drew half of a Red Cross parcel and half a loaf of bread.

> Started bargaining with civilians. Soap and cigarettes . . . dropped off to side to cook. Four of us made a big pot of oatmeal and eggs in a driving rain. Good eating.

He and colleague Dunlap 'looked after' an ailing guard and carried his gun. 'What a war!' He notes dryly. They stopped and asked a housewife for a bed, saying they were ill. 'She gave us a room all to ourselves. Plenty of straw, hot water, fire, potatoes and brot. Ate, dried our clothes and went to bed.'

Mike's diary records 'amusing incidents looting milk-churns whilst straggling'. His mates Don and Frank 'hopped a truck', so Michael joined up with Conk Canton, Geoff Cornish and 'Pop' Coventry. Mike's diary describes Conk:

> He was the Intelligence Officer at Sagan. He was security conscious to the extreme: it was alleged that he was the man Our Lord had in mind when he said, 'His left hand knoweth not what his right hand doeth'. He was not allowed to join

> the escapers from Sagan owing to his security knowledge. I think he must have been ill at the time Sagan was evacuated.

The four subsequently became known – at least to themselves – as 'The Firm' and quickly functioned as the classic, well-oiled machine:

> We left the column at 1700 hours and approached some women at Piebarce in order to stay in their barn. Geoff got to work and we were soon being served by them in their parlour. During the meal two goons arrived, which threatened to alter things. One announced that he'd be court-martialled if he'd walked another step. Geoff considered dosing them – they leave.

After a period of whatever-on-earth Geoff's intervention involved: 'We stay'.

When scrounging rubbish from the garbage heap at a farm, The Firm found the remains off an old twisted pram chassis, with only its four wheels, frame and underchassis left. The rubber had been burnt off the tyres in a fire. They grabbed it. They straightened it as best they could, found some old planks and secured them on the frame with rubber bands where the springs would have originally joined the chassis to the undercarriage. It was christened 'Cuthbert'. They plaited a little bit of rope from the string from their parcels and anchored that to the front of the chassis as a substitute for its long-departed handle. When anyone pulled the string, Cuthbert went all over the place, until someone would pull their string to get it back on the road. Cuthbert's steering was effected by achieving a fine balance between a number of pieces of string and their attached humans. The Firm strapped all their belongings, including their four packs, onto Cuthbert. They were now free of their overburden, and 'crabbed' on. Michael recalls:

> We had quite a bit to carry as we had the camp medical supplies, including a sack of kaolin for stopping 'the squitters'. I used to get annoyed with Geoff and Pop for saying 'we pushed it from Nurnberg to Moosburg' – I reckon I did all the pushing, while they were somewhere in the column gassing and prescribing. It was quite a long way: I think I measured it at 92 miles. I learnt afterwards that our pram contained the Sagan (secret) wireless. If true, I was mighty glad I didn't know it at the time.

On 7 April they strapped the box of goodies onto Cuthbert and had gone about seventeen kilometres when they had to climb a very long steep hill. 'Cuthbert capsized, which necessitated modifications to lower the centre of gravity.' On arriving at Beilngries at midday they found about thirty of the men from their own Block, already there. Mike continues:

> Geoff seduces Russian girl. Spent night in barn. Blood curdling scream at night when Smith fell through floor of barn. Acquired a hammer and some pruning scissors out of an engine-house.

On 8 April they crossed the Danube, 'which did look blue from certain angles'. After a few days morale heightened visibly. The weather was now hot, and every time the marchers went through a town they polished their buttons, whistled and sang their way through the centre in step, everybody with their shoulders back to demonstrate their high spirits and to demoralise the local population as much as they could. When they stopped for the night they bedded themselves down in barns and if anyone could get some hay they were very pleased. They got into the cattle yards and sheds which were beautifully warm. 'Moreover, you had to work out which was the wrong end of the cow, or you could be in big trouble during the night – and a couple of times, blokes were,' Geoff recalls.

Around Neustadt the men encountered some hostility from elements of the Nazi 15 Panzer Division. They camped in a sports field, brewed tea and watched a Thunderbolt attack at close hand. Following this scrap of relaxation they were threatened with being bundled into a train as punishment for their straggling. They had all been in cattle trucks before and marched a further five kilometres to Muhlhausen after dark. On the way Mike received an astronomy lecture from Pop and The Firm spent another night in a barn.

Over ensuing days Mike's diary tells that: his watch spring broke; they bypassed Pfeffenhausen to avoid the Wehrmacht; they drew parts of some American parcels; and they passed 'quite a few ineffectual tank barriers'.

On 10 April they had a pleasant day. 'Stole a [beer] Steiner out of an inn. Firm's stock now a loaf and 14 eggs.' In 2004, at the time of writing, Michael still has the Steiner and indeed his single page diary. At Gammelsdorf they stocked up with potatoes stolen from pigfood supplies, mangels (a beet grown for animal fodder), and flour. Geoff and Pop continued to move along the column and look after the sick men each night.

During the day, Geoff would go into a farmhouse and engage the farmer, his wife and their kids, and say that they were looking for food, for anything. That on a farm, they must have 'a little bit' left over:

> I'd keep the whole family there while my mates were round the back ratting the kitchen. Then back into the column and the farmer would finally say:

> 'Nein, ich habe nichts . . . I've got nothing I can give you.'
>
> I'd say: 'you're probably right', because when they went back into the house again, everything that was edible, moveable or of any value, had gone.

The men supplemented their supplies quite well along the route with this practice which they described as 'living off the land'. Later Pop Coventry stopped a French POW driving a wagon. The Postern (guard who watched the rear end of the column) shooed the Frenchman on saying the men only stopped him to steal things from his cart. The Frenchman winked and moved on, whereupon the Postern halted him and handed him back a pot.

The prisoners continued to have contact with England with their clandestine radios, but at this stage learnt little from that source. They were simply focused on keeping alive. Wenthe's diary describes the ways in which things were changing: 'had run of the house, guards living next to us – we helped them cook. Chatted a bit and then to bed again'. He adds: 'rumours aplenty; kriegies' stories astounding – a movie of this would be priceless'.

On April 13, when almost at Munich, Michael records: 'Roosevelt died. Red Cross trucks arrive'.

Geoff tells us:

> That morning, Cuthbert was straggling along when a great dust cloud appeared above the road ahead. The dust was raised by a convoy of trucks. The column was ordered off the road to allow it to pass. The trucks had red crosses all over them. When the convoy stopped, the men went to investigate, asking:
>
> 'What's this?'
>
> 'Supplies!' All for you'

'For us???'
'Yes!'

The story was that the Allies had to get supplies, including the Red Cross parcels, into Switzerland which was the key neutral country and the clearing house for the movement of goods. The Swiss Red Cross took charge of the incoming goods there, but Germany had responsibility for distribution to the camps. The latter could do little because they had no resources, no trucks or any vehicle that could move the supplies. Ever since, vast reserves had been building up in Switzerland.

The men learnt later that an American based in Switzerland, had donated the convoy of trucks to the Swiss Red Cross with a commitment to pay volunteer Swiss drivers to take them across the frontier. Anything, to move the supplies to where they were needed. The 'top American driver rates' were of course a fortune – in the order of a year's salary for a week's work. Geoff remains surprised and disappointed to this day that the American was never identified or able to be thanked for his generosity. Geoff says:

> The men just couldn't believe what was happening! All these supplies. As well as food, the trucks were laden with medical goods: sulphanilamides, antiseptics, antacids and bandages! Everyone broke down and wept – unashamedly bawling their eyes out.

After being the underdog for so long, suddenly, as if from the heavens, all this bounty had come.

X–X–X–X–X–X–X

From then on the 'prisoners' had command of the situation. They were still prisoners but the guards were on their side now. At the end of every day's march, the medicos would look after the guards and the villagers.

On the same day as Roosevelt's death and the trucks' arrival on 13 April 1945, the front of the column reached the old town of Moosburg outside Munich, where the march ended. Mike's diary records:

> Goons brought up some soup and overturned the wagon whilst turning in the road. Stole a ladle, which Goons discovered on Cuthbert. Conk was called 'schweinhund' and was nearly struck by said wrathful goon.

They stopped outside Moosburg town and brewed tea. At the Moosburg camp they were relieved to evade being searched, and each had a shower. There were over 300 men per tent. There were far too few tents and many prisoners slept outside. Shanty buildings were constructed, sanitation was appalling, and yet again there were only two taps for the whole contingent. The German forces were in full retreat and General Patton was pursuing them mightily. The prisoners now knew from their secret radios that he was getting close.

One morning there was a lot of noisy gunfire around the camp. Everyone kept very quiet, low and still. The next thing was a crash and a couple of American tanks flattened the front gates. All the guards had gone by then, most having fled about half an hour earlier because they did not want to be captured and taken prisoner. Glemnitz' later communications reveal that he was quick to move his men out, to avoid as long as possible their being captured. The now-free allied men ripped holes in the wire around the camp and burst through the electrified fences. Some were killed instantly.

As most of these marchers were American air crew, there was great jubilation when they saw the stars on the tanks. The Americans brought through a doughnut van. Everyone stuffed themselves. Geoff vomited. The food was too rich. 'We were of course just beside ourselves. We just could not believe it was true.'

'I wasn't there long after that because somebody yelled "any medical personnel here?" They were speechless with what they'd seen.' Having no idea what was in store, Geoff was the only respondent. 'Get in! Come,' he was bidden.

13

WITNESSING HOLOCAUST

The excited Americans took Geoff to the Dachau concentration camp, which had just been liberated. He arrived simultaneously with the first officials and the press. Geoff describes:

> That was the worst scene I can ever remember; I never want to see anything like it again. Heaps of bulldozed bodies some moving, some not, some had had diesel poured over them, and there was still the odd flicker of flames at the edges. We went through them, put those on stretchers who showed any sign of life when we touched or looked at them. Some of them were dying on the stretchers. We took them back to the camp and showered them. After that they were taken away, presumably to a hospital.
>
> To see that look of incredible disbelief, relief in somebody who was so ill that they virtually had nothing left, but they clung to life so fiercely you could see that they knew now that . . . it was all worthwhile, there was hope.

And today:

> If anyone talks to me about euthanasia they get very short shrift. I could never bring myself to take another person's life deliberately, particularly as a doctor. Relieve all the suffering

> and the pain but work to . . . That did make an enormous impression on me. Everything was in utter turmoil.

He continues:

> And then another group of Americans grabbed me and took me in a tank. They raced through the southeast, about ten or twelve kilometres into the forest and said 'there's a clearing in there with some huts in it and a couple of hundred Hitler youth inside. Would you tell them in German to come out with their hands up.'

Geoff did as he was asked. The reply was: 'Come and get us'.

> This group of Americans, at that moment, having already liberated the concentration camp, were in no mood to do anything slowly. They backed the tanks off, levelled the guns, and blew the lot out of existence. There were no survivors.

He concludes by acknowledging that it was another black day, about which he could do nothing: 'I had no say in it.'

Later, as many reports describe, General Patton came and mingled among the men. Mike Horsfall recalls this being on 1 May, after the May Day March for the 27 Russian Generals. Geoff did not himself witness Patton's speech because he was at the time engaged in the expeditions described above. Durand relates:

> General Patton arrived in his command car . . . not the dull green usually seen at the front, but brightly shined and suitably decorated with sirens, spotlights, and a four-star flag . . . then mounted the hood of the car to speak.
>
> The prisoners crowded around . . . a respectful three or

> four feet away, and no one touched the command car. Patton . . . addressed the crowd . . . and saw a Nazi flag still flying. Pointing toward it, he said: 'I want that son-of-a-bitch cut down . . . I guess all you sons-a-bitches are glad to see me' . . . a great roar went up. After the noise died down, he went on: 'I'd like to stay with you awhile, but I've got a date with a woman in Munich, it's 40 kilometres away, and I've got to fight every damned inch of the way. God bless you and thank you for what you've done.'

Just as dusk was falling, German aircraft came in from the East to surrender to the Americans rather than to the Russians. They were flying white streamers out of the back of the assortment of Junkers and other craft, right up to the modern Fokker. One came in with his streamer behind him, pressed his firing button, and blasted the line of tanks on the road. They shot him down straight away; he was only about two hundred feet above the ground.

The non-American prisoners perceived that these new troops wanted to 'shoot down everything' so that they wouldn't have to 'go back to Mummy in the States without really tasting war'. The prisoners raced over to the American gunners and demanded they stop.

> We just got physical with them, I think we hurt a few people, but we just couldn't bear to stand by and see people getting shot down, when they were actually on their landing approach to surrender. They would have only been two or three minutes from being in their hands.

When it came time for the liberated prisoners repatriation, they were taken by truck to Landshut aerodrome where they camped to wait for the Douglas DC-3s which would ferry them to

Rheims. They were at Landshut on the night of VE day, 8 May. They went to a grass airstrip to wait for the DC-3 Dakotas, 'goony birds', as the Americans called them. The plan was that from Rheims, the RAF personnel would board Lancasters; the Americans, Super Fortresses. Eight DC3 Dakotas were expected. The first seven were lined up wing tip to wing tip. The men begged: 'For God's sake don't do that – this is a grass airstrip, there's a big muddy patch and if the next one in hits the muddy patch he'll slew around and clean up all the others.'

The organisers' attitude was 'shut up, we're doing this'. They wouldn't listen to any advice. Sure enough the eighth aircraft came in, skidded around, clipped with his port wing the wingtips of the whole seven parked aircraft and flipped them – all were rendered completely unserviceable, including his own.

'There's no concrete there, only mud' . . . 'well goddam,' they said. Geoff comments dryly: 'As they say, you can always tell an American – but not much!'

That incident delayed the men's return to England; they didn't arrive until 10 May. VE day was 8 May, so they missed all the celebrations – they were still waiting in the old huts at Landshut aerodrome. It took them another two days to reach Britain and on 10 May they reached Rheims. Before they would step into the Lancasters, they demanded: 'How many hours flying have you done?' of the smiling, young Canadian pilot. They weren't going to go with a rookie!

×–×–×–×–×–×–×

That was where Geoff said goodbye to his American friends including Brewster Morgan, whose parting words were an invitation to visit Hawaii. 'Sure, Brews,' retorted Geoff, as if it were just across the road.

Geoff says that the men couldn't stop grinning, ear to ear. Shouting, hooray, hooray. He remembers the trip well:

> There were no seats or anything; you just sat on the floor in the bomb bay, in the belly of the plane. It was so noisy, right there next to the engines – all right there just feet from your head.

So different from any of their previous flights. When they arrived in England, they were deloused:

> Oh dear, blowing DDT dust into you everywhere – you wouldn't touch it now and we were peppered with it. We had everything that crawled walked or scratched; lice, bedbugs, crabs – if it walked or bit, we had it. A good shower and then all our clothing was dumped and burnt! So we landed back without any souvenirs, like the day we were born! We were given passes to wherever we wanted to go on our disembarkation leave. What a feeling of relief, to be free to go.

And then:

> If you wanted to turn left, you could turn left, you could turn right if you wanted to turn right. You could stop still if you wanted to and no one could put a bayonet or a gun up to you and say that 'you can't do that'.

RAF personnel were given recreational leave which accrued, for overseas personnel, to a day for every month you'd been away from home, 61 days for being a POW and another day for every month of imprisonment. Geoff had a huge wad of leave waiting, because he had spent almost 50 months as a prisoner of war.

14

Go past go

As soon as the men arrived back in Britain, they were kitted out with civilian clothes and allowed to go on leave. Geoff was entitled to around six months leave on the basis of the RAF formula. He immediately returned to stay with the Bryants who were dedicated to restoring him to good health and as always, insisted that their home was his home. He was tired, unwell and weighed only 38 kilogrammes. He spent a few blissful days sleeping and eating and was then presented with a 'baby' Austin car in which he could go wherever he pleased. Having scrounged some fuel – which was of course rationed and in very short supply, he made his way off. He was meandering along a quiet country road when a Belgian Army lorry, speeding around a corner on the wet tarmac, skidded across and pinned his car to the abutting brick wall. The Austin was shortened by about a foot and the driver was crushed inside.

Three days later, Geoff awoke in the Stratford on Avon hospital and found himself with an injured left knee and a broken right hand enclosed in a plaster cast. The car was a write off but the Bryants didn't mind in the least: their friend was fine and the car had been insured. Again, Geoff was lucky to be alive. Attempting to rehabilitate himself, Geoff found that he was able to write quite easily with his left hand. His father's unwelcome early training had rendered him ambidextrous, at least in handwriting.

His injuries entitled Geoff to a further period of leave to recover, so he decided to go to London to collect his mail and read the papers at Australia House. He caught up with friends including fellow pilot Tim Newman who had just been to New Zealand House. Tim had heard that anyone who'd been a prisoner of war was allowed to take their sixty one days special leave at their home address, if they intended to continue with their service in the RAF. Although Geoff had not intended to continue in the RAF, he was not going to miss out on any leave he could wangle. He went immediately to the Air Ministry to make further enquiries, and there found another mate, Malcolm McColm, also an Australian and an ex-POW. Malcolm would later become a Queensland Member of Parliament back home. 'I've just heard about this wonderful leave' Geoff spluttered, 'at home, and I want some!' Malcolm knew what the deal was and happily obliged. Geoff left with a 'wonderful letter' on RAF Headquarters' stationery. The letter stated that Geoff was entitled to sixty one days' leave at his home address, and that he could travel, with top priority, by any means available. At public expense! Malcolm emphasised the value of taking a circuitous route because travel time was additional to the time spent at home: 'Here, bum your way around the world' were his parting words.

Geoff skipped out of the Ministry, delighted. After going back to the Bryants' for a few more days, he made his way to Southampton to look for a passage to Australia. The ship *Alcantara* with Canadian flashes on the side was in port, waiting to sail for Canada. Geoff wandered up the gangplank and showed his 'magic pass' to the officer in charge:

'Got a spot for me mate?'

'No, we're full up.'

'You must have one somewhere.'

However, as the officer realised the import of the magic pass: 'Well, I suppose, if you can find a berth . . .' 'I'll find a berth alright!'

So the ship sailed with Geoff on board, along with 600 Canadian Air Force officers on their way home. Before leaving he wrote a brief letter to Gitte in Denmark explaining that he was going to Australia but would be back soon. After arriving at Halifax, Newfoundland, Geoff caught a train to Montreal where he was entertained by a Canadian Scheme similar to the Lady Frances Ryder one in Britain. He was in no hurry to get back to Australia and even less to return to England or the RAF. As far as he was concerned, world travel was a very attractive part of the deal. The feeling of freedom was unbelievable, incomparable. The joy of being able to do what he liked, when he liked after four years' imprisonment! Being in new places, meeting new people, eating fresh tasty food. His host family in Montreal was named Jacquay and they had a daughter, just Geoff's age. War was still underway in the Pacific. On August 14, shortly after Geoff's arrival in Montreal, Japan sued for surrender. The place went absolutely wild. There were parties everywhere. Geoff enjoyed the celebrations for a few days and then moved on, catching a train south to Washington from whence by air to San Diego.

x–x–x–x–x–x–x

There were no immediate connecting flights out so he proceeded to investigate San Diego. He surfed on beautiful beaches, which he judged to be no better than those at home in Perth.

He met some Americans in a bar who asked had he been to Mexico. 'Come on, we'll take you. It's not far to Tijuana.' So he and his new friends piled into a car, talking all the way and headed south. When they reached the border, the Americans brought out their American identity papers and Geoff his tickets and 'Letter'. The border guard was unimpressed:

'Where's your pass?'

'Not a fucking letter, your fucking PASS!'

The Americans argued, 'But . . . '

'No PASS, no entry! I don't care if you reverse back up the road and write it out yourself!'

So they did.

Returning with the quickly improvised pass, the men were not only allowed to proceed, but were saluted by the guard as they crossed the border. So much easier than forging a passport in Stalag Luft III. They had an enjoyable day in Tijuana and returned to San Diego that evening. Next morning Geoff again boarded an RAF Transport Command aircraft, for his next destination, Hickham Military Airfield, Hawaii.

Never having dreamed that he might be able to take up Brewster Morgan's invitation to visit Hawaii, Geoff was ecstatic to now be able to contact his friend. They had occupied adjacent rooms in North Camp, met again in Nuremberg, and parted ways after liberation. Brewster was one of the many Americans who couldn't wait for America to join in the war, and had gone to Canada to sign up with the Royal Canadian Air Force. These Americans were known as the 'Eagle Squadron' of the RCAF and, in deference to their own country, wore the American Eagle as a flash on their shoulders.

Geoff found a phone and rang Brewster:

'It's me, Geoff.'

'Where the hell are you?'

'Hickham!'

'How long ya here?'

'Six hours.'

'SIX HOURS! I can't show you Hawaii in six hours. I'll be right there.'

Brewster arrived in his father's Packard. 'We'll have to have a flat tyre at Kahuku Point. It's about a hundred miles north of here, the northernmost point of Oahu Island.' The men headed for Kahuku, Geoff marvelling at the scenery and the sight of sunken battleships' masts sticking up out of the water. He was enthralled. This was the original hell hole of war in the Pacific.

Brews timed the trip beautifully, pulling the Packard up outside the airport just as Geoff's aircraft left the ground. The Australian raced from the car and stumbled in puffing and panting, as the plane disappeared into the sky.

The Canadian Officer in charge, of similar rank to Geoff, was furious. 'Cornish, where were you when the aircraft took off?' he barked.

'We had a flat tyre at the other end of Oahu.'

'You can stay here and starve and ROT, you bastard!'

'But . . . what will I do for money?' pleaded the miscreant.

'That's your problem!' He didn't want to know.

Geoff breathed a sigh of relief, kept a straight face, and went back around the corner to the Packard. 'Indefinite leave, Brews!' 'Great.'

They went off to begin partying. Brewster took his friend home to the family's mansion with its black marble floors and hot and cold running servants. The servants were all Japanese Americans who had been there since long before the war. Geoff was welcomed into the family, had his own guest wing and became part of the victory celebrations all over the island. Brewster had been born in Hawaii. His father was a retired surgeon and had recently suffered a stroke; he loved Brewster and Geoff to chat with him about their war experiences. Brewster had a galaxy of invitations to parties both because of his own return and because of the imminent signing of the Surrender. He would ring his friends and say:

> 'Of course I'd love to come to the yachting party, if I can bring my Australian buddy?'
>
> 'Sure, you can bring your Australian Buddy.'

They had a ball. It was a level of excitement and luxury that Geoff had never experienced in Australia or even in Britain. He was really fit, surfing every day, partying every night and the Japanese surrender was about to be signed! Heaven.

One of Brewster's closest friends was the Commanding Officer at Hickham Military Airfield. The men would go in and Brewster would ask: 'Got any aircraft you aren't using this morning?' 'Sure Brews, there's that one over there.' It would usually be an old Douglas Dive Bomber, which Brewster was quite happy to pilot. They were outdated craft which Geoff had never even seen before. So off the pair would fly, courtesy of the USAAF, to visit the other Hawaiian Islands. Many of Brewster's Dad's friends had their own airstrips at locations right across the archipelago.

The pair spent a lot of time at the Officers' Club at Hickham and were there on September 2, when the news came through that the Surrender had finally been signed. Geoff giggles: 'I remembered that day well, the next day a little and the third day, not at all. What a party!'

A couple of days later, in the early evening Geoff, Brewster and a couple of girls were walking up the steps of the Royal Hawaiian Hotel, the 'Pink Palace of the Pacific'. Coming down was the Canadian Air Force officer, who immediately recognised Geoff, obviously far from 'starving and rotting'. The officer removed his hat, threw it on the ground and stamped on it, his face and neck crimson and the arteries protruding on his forehead: 'Cornish, you bastard, I'll move you out tomorrow in a landing barge to Australia!'

Brewster muttered: 'I think he's a bit definite!' So the men took their leave, went back to Hickham and asked Brewster's friend whether there were any aircraft due to depart in the direction of Australia.

> 'Yes, there's one but it's full, it's RAF Transport Command, shuttling people from Hawaii to Australia.'
>
> 'That'll be perfect!'

Geoff decided to push his luck: 'I thought I'd better get home now, so I got on board and showed my magic pass. There was an [army] brigadier who had A1 priority.' Geoff also had A1 priority. Because the Command was Air Force, not Army, and Geoff's 'magic letter' was likewise, our hero was able to 'pull rank' on the brigadier. 'He was a bit upset because I got his seat, but that didn't matter to me. I'd had a glorious time.' Had the flight been Army Transport Command, Geoff would have had no hope of such a result.

The trip to Sydney was not to be quick. A few hours into the flight the aircraft developed an engine fault and was forced to land in Fiji. It was ten days before a new engine arrived, during which interlude the passengers spent a lot of their time in the Officers' Mess at Nadi. Eventually they resumed their flight to Sydney. Every time there was another delay at Fiji, Geoff says, 'I telegrammed my mother who cancelled the party and ate all the cakes'. Eventually he was able to communicate that he would definitely be reaching Sydney 'tonight!'

'Mum asked my ninety-year-old great aunt Polly and Edna, her spinster daughter of fifty six, to organise my stay in Sydney.' He expected to be there for a day or two before flying on to Perth. In all of his eighteen years in Western Australia, he had never been to Sydney, and he could not wait to see the night life and the legendary surf beaches. The delay in Fiji had only served to intensify his excitement.

When the plane landed in Sydney there was an instruction for no one to stand or leave the plane. There appeared to be an emergency.

A Nursing Sister in uniform came down the aisle and stopped in front of Geoff:

> 'Flight Lieutenant Cornish?'
>
> 'Yes' Geoff answered, puzzled.
>
> '*You're* the Prisoner of War?'
>
> 'Er, yes.'
>
> 'You look alright to me!'
>
> 'I'm great!'
>
> 'We were ordered to bring an ambulance for you!'

Great-Aunt Polly had not understood the difference between the injured POWs who were being repatriated from Japan since the surrender, and her very fit and healthy young relative.

'I disposed of the nursing sister very quickly,' Geoff concludes. He then found that his troubles were really only beginning. Polly and Edna took Geoff home, fed him a good meal and expected to be regaled with stories of adventure. They were probably not disappointed but Geoff was. The night out on the town which he had looked forward to all the way from Fiji, was not to be. He had a pocket full of money, was in good spirits and had never before been to Sydney. The ladies eventually decided to retire and showed Geoff to his room. He breathed a sigh of relief and prepared to escape through the window, because the ladies lay sleeping between him and the front and only door.

Further frustration waited. He was a captive again. When

he leaned out the window to effect his escape, he found that he was at the top of a cliff. Beneath him was a sheer drop into darkness. He could not tell exactly how far down the ground was, but it was clearly a long way. He thus spent his only night in Sydney, safely snuggled down in a little bed at the top of a cliff. The next morning he flew out for Perth, to home, rationing and a very excited family.

The spring wildflowers in Kings Park were a picture.

15

PLANNING A FUTURE

Many things had changed. Most significantly, his brother Keith was dead. The chasm this left in the family was a loss from which Dot and Fred would never recover. His next brother Gordon was now aged nineteen, his sister Audrey fourteen and the youngest, Roy, twelve. They were almost like two families. Geoff had been away so long and Keith's absence created such a dichotomy between the present, and his remembered, reality.

Everyone was delighted to see Geoff back home, a veritable return of a prodigal son. His parents bloomed with pride: 'My son Geoff,' Fred would announce at every opportunity. Gordon and Geoff were so alike that Dot would often confuse them: 'Which one of you is it now?' The euphoria of the end of the war was only surpassed by the joy of reunion. Fred took Geoff to see William, Geoff's grandfather, now old and frail, who died on 8 November, soon after seeing his long-absent grandson.

Geoff went about renewing old acquaintances and friendships. He recalls that the first person he sought out was Professor Noel Bayliss, who had been so good to him during the 'Cadet' days, closely followed by Ivor Hanger, his former YMCA mentor.

He set about working out how he could organise his medical training. He called into Air Force headquarters in Perth and the man in charge of rations and passes turned out to be fellow classmate Johnno from Perth Boys', who said that he could organise food, coupons, and travel for his friend.

It was so good to be back to the surf and the bush. Geoff hadn't really danced since before the war and decided to take private lessons with 'Piranthione' a classy dancing school. Never one to stint when opportunity presented itself, he had personal classes four times per day, until he considered that he had gained sufficient skill.

While Geoff was at home his sister Audrey was required to write an essay for school, on the subject of 'conjuring'. Geoff regaled her with his stories of 'Bush' Parker and the Gestapo. Audrey was open mouthed, as was her English master when he read her rendition of the story. 'It was the only time Geoff ever told me anything about life in the prison camps,' she says. 'The teacher just couldn't take his eyes off the page!'

Geoff spent several months in and out of Perth. During that time he went to Adelaide and Melbourne on the 'free' RAAF transport, just waving 'The Letter'. He organised everything for his long dreamed of medical course – he would be required to re-enrol for first year Science in Perth then transfer to Melbourne for the rest of the training. He was terribly anxious to just get on with the course, but had to go back to England to be demobilised.

In November he decided to contact the RAF Base in Melbourne about returning to Britain, given that he hadn't heard a word from them during his entire stay. He received a very terse reply that stated that his letter was the first they knew of his presence in Australia. They required 'some indication of how and when you arrived in this country'.

'They wanted me out pretty quickly.' So he went back to his friend 'Johnno'. 'I just want to get back to England.' Johnno organised a flight out, and Geoff left for Colombo.

Colombo was the very last stop on the RAF run from San

Diego. Passengers then took an RAF domestic flight from the colony of Colombo to the UK. At the time aircraft couldn't take off in England because of snow and foul weather. There was a huge backlog of 'high priority' passengers waiting to get back to England.

Geoff was disconsolately cooling his heels in the transit officers' mess, with a quiet drink. There was a wing commander on the next stool. He said:

> 'Cornish, you don't remember me do you?'
>
> 'No sir, I'm sorry I don't.'
>
> 'I was a Sergeant under you at Cranwell in 1940.'
>
> 'You seem to be doing fairly well,' Geoff replied.
>
> 'Yes, I'm Mountbatten's Chief of Air Staff out here. What are you doing?'
>
> 'Twiddling my thumbs on my way back to England.'
>
> 'Oh,' he said, 'we'll get a garry and take you out to our Mess.'

The Mess was situated in the middle of town, right next to the top class Galle Face Hotel. It was a beautiful Mess. They had set themselves up magnificently. They said, 'We've got a Christmas dance tonight but there are hardly any girls around.'

Geoff went off to spend the day surfing and sunbaking. 'There were five pretty girls messing about in the shallow water, giggling, getting themselves wet and throwing water.' Geoff quickly moved closer:

> I went out – I'd been surfing in Hawaii and at home, and I came in on a wave and cleaned up about three of them. I listened to them talk and they were Dutch. I spoke to them in German. I said 'I'm Australian but what are you girls doing here?'

> They were Dutch nurses going to New Guinea, but there were problems there and they'd been forbidden to proceed. They were out to have a bit of a good time before they had to go 'back to Mum', in a conservative, Catholic country. So I asked them to come to the party that night.
>
> I walked into the Christmas party with four beautiful Dutch blondes on my arm. That blew them away!

Eventually Geoff managed to reach England and reported to RAF headquarters to request discharge. First, he was asked in which branch of the RAF he wished to continue his service. He explained that he had changed his mind and really wanted to return home to Australia. His masters were not impressed – they were in fact quite hostile. So Geoff twitched. He twitched again, and staggered as though he might be about to fall over. He twitched again. His seniors drew breath and appeared to reconsider. They acceded to his request. He was told that he would have to attend a POW resettlement centre while a passage to Australia was being arranged, and that his rehabilitation should focus on the development of skills for his future. He was sent to a resettlement centre at Rugby, between Coventry and Birmingham and asked what he wanted to do. While there he again followed up on old contacts:

> As soon as I arrived back in England I again contacted Gitte, the Danish girl with whom I had corresponded from the prison camp. I told her I wanted to visit her in Denmark, to ask her to marry me. She replied that she thought that I'd gone back to Australia for good, after I'd let her know that I was going there earlier. 'I'm married now,' she said.

Geoff tells us:

> I was devastated, so disappointed. Nevertheless I still wanted to meet her, to see this wonderful girl whom I had dreamed about, to meet her and her husband. 'I want to see you and complete the picture.'

He obtained a short period of leave.

> Gitte and her husband, a red headed Dane called Paddy, agreed that I could visit. They met me at the airport. I had the most wonderful few days. Paddy had been a member of the Resistance and took me everywhere, all around, to see the things that they'd done, the things they'd blown up. Eventually I said to her that I realised I'd messed things up, when I went to Australia. I gave her one kiss and of course I didn't contact her again.

Not too much later, he would meet another young lady who looked just like Gitte.

x–x–x–x–x–x–x

At Rugby an occupation was eventually found for Geoff. He had steadfastly maintained his intention to study medicine and emphasised that moreover, he had already made provision to enrol in first year, in Australia. The rehabilitation system was that men would be placed in employment of the type they wished to follow in the future, free of charge to the employer, with the trainee being paid his full air force salary. The employer would gain a worker, albeit an 'apprentice' and the trainee would learn on the job skills. There were unlimited opportunities with so many of Britain's adult workers still in the Army of Occupation in Europe or in the Far East. It was not readily obvious what might be done with Geoff, with his medical experience from the prison camps but not a certificate of any kind, not even first aid. The officer responsible for his placement had once attended a local private, secondary school, the 'Lawrence Sheriff' School. He phoned the school: 'Could we send this young man to join the sixth form?' His charge could attend school with the sixth formers and follow the science syllabus which was very similar to that of first year university. Botany, biology, chemistry and physics – more revision for Geoff.

So Geoff acquired more civilian clothes and attended school with the eighteen year olds. 'I'd read my schoolbooks in the bus and was dropped off at the Sheriff School to do my lessons with the sixth formers.' When the school learned of his fluency in German, he was permitted to teach a class. The bus from Rugby back to the RAF Base didn't leave until 5.30 pm so he took his rugger boots in and did training between 3.30 and 5.00. He would then catch the bus back to the RAF Base, change into uniform and have dinner in the Mess with his mates.

The sixth formers invited Geoff to practise rugby with them when they realised that he had played before. Geoff joined them and after a few weeks the school had a match coming up against Rugby School. They said: 'we haven't got a scrum half – will you play? This really will be your last year enrolled at a school!' So Geoff played rugby at Rugby against Rugby!

x–x–x–x–x–x–x

The boys from the Base would go into Coventry for entertainment, which they knew well from before the war. The city was in the early stages of reconstruction following its almost complete destruction. He recalls that in early April 1945:

> I knew all the dance halls and pubs from training days in 1940. I went to a dance hall and there were these beautiful girls everywhere, dancing with each other. There were no English guys around. There were about forty or fifty couples and only about six men!

For an ex-POW it was a smorgasbord! I spotted two gorgeous blondes and went up to them and asked 'may I break you up and have this dance?' They looked at each other and said 'yes'. We danced and I introduced myself. She said 'I'm Myra' then she went and sat down.

Geoff thought for a moment. So many pretty girls. He followed Myra to her seat:

> 'May I have the next dance?'
>
> 'Yes.' She said.
>
> 'The next dance?'
>
> 'Yes.'
>
> 'The next dance?'
>
> 'Yes.'
>
> 'The next dance?'
>
> 'No, I've got to sit down. I get too puffed. I've got a bad heart.'

Geoff had been taking Myra out for about three weeks when she got a job at Bournemouth as a hotel receptionist. The rest quickly became history. He tells us what happened:

> She was ideal for the job – so pretty, blonde, with a lovely figure and as bright as bright can be. I went down to visit her one Sunday, had a lovely day and we went to bathe on the beach. The die was cast. I was in love. The sunlight and sand did for me what moonlight and roses did for an Englishman.

> Before I knew where I was, I'd lost my freedom and my clothing coupons. She'd said, 'Ooh, yes!'

Geoff went back to the base that night, straight to the Mess and said, 'I've got engaged!' The others shouted: 'open the bar!' The men all went to breakfast next morning straight from there.

While he was in Bournemouth that weekend, a message had been received for the now newly-committed young man. 'Sailing sailing, over the ocean main – my sailing orders for Australia had come through.'

Geoff was required to report to Uxbridge, near London, to be discharged from the RAF on the following Saturday. His ship was to sail on Sunday. He rang and checked about taking Myra but found that the government would pay a passage only for a wife, not a fiancée. Oh dear!

He raced to the registry office in Coventry. He had to be forty eight hours in the city before being permitted to marry. It was now 10.00 am Monday [*17 May*], so Wednesday morning at ten would be the earliest possible marriage booking. He took out a licence and raced the few blocks to the Lloyd-Evans's place, to speak to Myra's father.

> 'Pop, I'm in love with your daughter.'
>
> 'Yes we know that.'
>
> 'I'd like to marry her.'
>
> 'Yes.'
>
> 'You mean that?'
>
> 'Yes of course.'

Geoff continues:

> 'I was always pulling his leg – How about 10.30 Wednesday morning? Here's the licence!'

> Well, Pop sort of collapsed in a heap and I rang Myra. I said: 'Grab the next train to come back' – then another person collapsed in a heap. She came, and I met her at the station at Coventry. On the next day, the Tuesday, we had to arrange a reception and her outfit, everything.

Geoff thought he should telegram his parents. He did so: 'Engaged to Myra. Getting married Wednesday. Sail for home Sunday'. They replied: 'Myra who?' The family were completely shocked but recall the news as such 'typical Geoff'.

The boys at the RAF Mess allowed Geoff to take whatever he wanted from the bar and put it on his bill, on the basis that he could return what was not used. Coventry was in pieces. Dressmakers were scattered all over the city in people's private homes. The couple traipsed around and found a hat in one place, a dress in another, gloves somewhere else. They then went to the Gaumont theatre where Geoff had seen so many films in his training days, for a cup of tea. There was a function room available which they could hire for a reception, and the Gaumont proprietors were able to organise the food, without coupons!

The Bryants were quickly contacted and Mrs Bryant was delighted to attend. As she lived so close to Coventry, it was easy for her to be there, although Colonel Bryant was unable to leave the farm. Mrs Bryant was the official witness to the marriage, the signatory on the couple's marriage certificate on 15 May 1946.

The Bryants insisted that Myra and Geoff spend the first night of their honeymoon at Goldicote. 'The old Colonel brought our breakfast in with a big wink the next morning! We had to rush out of the huge four poster bed and be driven to Stratford station to go straight down to London.'

Geoff spent Thursday and Friday being demobilised from the air force at Uxbridge, and going out at night with Myra. Myra saw her new husband off on Sunday morning to sail for Australia, and went back to her job at Bournemouth.

16

Marriage, Myra and medicine

Geoff sailed back to Australia aboard the *Stirling Castle*. The vessel quickly became known as the Starving Castle owing to the poor food served – so different from Geoff's previous trip all those years ago on the *Orama*. On board were some 600 – mostly English – brides of Australian servicemen. Jack Slatter and his wife were there, as was Kent Hughes with his new wife, and several others from the *Orama*.

All these British girls roaming around in the tiniest of short shorts! 'But I'd just been married and I wasn't interested.' It was generally a pleasurable trip for the men, 'no jobs to do, just catch up on books and loaf around'. When there was a 'Ladies Choice' at the dances, Geoff declares that he had to watch out. When the ship passed through the Suez Canal an aircraft carrier passed, going in the opposite direction. The men on board the carrier had been a year in the Far East and they almost swam to the *Castle*. Their envious ogling of the scantily dressed women everywhere on the decks moved Jack Slatter to yell 'for export only!' It was all great fun.

When Geoff arrived back in Australia in June he quickly settled into a routine with the family and with university. He resumed his science course and applied himself to his studies.

The family accommodated his anticipation of Myra's arrival although the date was still unknown. Various family members helped him prepare. He redecorated the bedroom which he and his brothers had shared so many years before. Gordon prepared an old second hand Indian motorcycle for Geoff and Myra's use – which would itself have some tales to tell. Grandma Cornish gave him a lovely old double bed.

In July, a telegram appeared from Myra, saying that she was on her way. Now that her anticipated arrival date was known, Dot and Fred began to plan a celebration. They hired the Supper Room at the local West Leederville Hall where Fred's RSL sub branch held their meetings, and prepared a wonderful wedding reception. She arrived on the first day of the August vacation so Geoff abandoned his studies and spent the vacation showing her around and showing her off. Although she didn't know a soul in Perth, one can only conclude that she would have had a very warm welcome.

Geoff declares that he doesn't know how he passed his exams that year, but the exposure he'd had to the material over so many years would have to have stood him in good stead.

They spent his vacation tearing around on the motorbike which Gordon had 'made roadworthy' for the couple. As they rounded a corner at speed, Geoff noticed that the motorbike was tilting one way and Myra was tilting the other. The sidecar began to vibrate and rattle, but didn't quite take off from the bike, so no one was injured. Geoff and Gordon each thought that the other had tightened the nuts which joined the sections together. During the break they visited Margaret River, Bunbury, Fremantle and other attractive parts of the southern tip of Western Australia.

All too soon, university recommenced and Geoff went back to his books. Life was generally fairly serious for him. He took Myra to dances and social events and a highlight was the University 'Freshmen's Ball'. He was again the Science Students' representative on the Student Union and met Shirley

Strickland, who represented the Arts students and would later become a legendary Olympian.

While Geoff was at university Myra mainly spent her time at home at Joseph Street. Her ability to explore Perth independently was hampered by her physical condition and lack of knowledge of people and the city itself. When Dot took Audrey and Myra shopping to Boans' Emporium to buy Audrey's school uniform, the salesman asked 'Which daughter is it for? 'I'll have you know I'm a married woman!' exclaimed Myra, feigning high dudgeon at being mistaken for a schoolgirl.

The rest of the year passed relatively without incident. Myra settled into the family, quickly had her father-in-law Fred 'around her little finger', and appears to have irritated Dot more than a little. While Myra's vivacious personality and flirtatious manner endeared her to many of those she met it seems to have been tiring for the immediate family. Her health was a major issue from the very start. Although she loved social life, she was constrained by low stamina. On seeking advice from a cardiologist about the prospect of children, Geoff and Myra were at this point simply told 'no'.

Once Geoff's first year science was completed in Perth it was time to transfer to Melbourne University's Faculty of Medicine. Much excitement. For Geoff it was the real beginning of his dream. For the rest of the family the final twenty four hours was the opportunity to vent the tensions of previous months. Mother and daughter-in-law 'had it out'. Fur and feathers flew, the family later admitted. One can only imagine the impact of the fiery, theatrical Myra on the otherwise quiet and well organised Cornish household.

x–x–x–x–x–x–x

The couple moved from Perth on the west coast of Australia to Melbourne in the south east and Geoff commenced his formal medical training. No more general sciences, but at last the core subjects of anatomy and physiology. Physiological experiments – testing the reflexes of a poor decerebrated frog and dissecting the cadavers of genuine, recently-deceased humans. One student was confronted in the passage of the anatomy building by a little old lady who wanted to know where she should go to donate her body. The young lady answered, and could only hope that the donation was not imminent.

The suburb of Surrey Hills was the couple's first Melbourne home, sharing with an old family friend, a retired post master general, Mr Page and his wife. They lived in James' Street, just before the tram terminus on Whitehorse Road where Melbourne's very last tram clock would bite the dust in the sixties. At James Street they had a part of a back verandah, enclosed by canvas blinds, with necessary furnishings and stored their suitcase under the bed. While living at James' Street, Geoff would cycle to the university each day – a good hour's ride each way, along either Barkers Road or Johnson Street to Carlton.

Geoff soon realised that his wife was indeed frail. 'She couldn't even push a carpet sweeper across a room without having to sit down,' he explains, 'so I just said alright I'll do the carpet sweeping'. 'She was just what I needed,' he continues. 'bright, cheerful and we were in love.' He believed that the steadying influence of his 'lovely wife' was critical to his successful completion of his medical course, both to prevent him from 'blowing my stack halfway through the course' and because she was happy to help with his study at home. What with studying non-stop before going to the war; having such a structured life in the RAF and then four years in POW camps, 'I really hadn't had a youth or any free time to myself'.

His days at the university were long and Myra was very pleased to see him home in the evening. There were even lectures on Saturday mornings. He didn't get to know the student body well because at day's end the others would all be off to the pub whilst Geoff couldn't wait to get home to Myra. He was amused at the student pranks and antics but they didn't come near what he had experienced in his days in the Stalag camps.

Geoff again established a study regime. In the evenings, he transcribed his lectures, referenced the information, committed it to memory then tested his recall. From the very beginning Myra was part of the routine. Geoff still suggests that she may have known as much about his subjects as he did. He would rise early and study again in the morning before leaving for university.

To make revision and testing easier, Geoff transferred a summary of the information for every topic and item, onto 'visiting cards' – little blocks of blank, white cardboard which he bought in bundles of one gross. For anatomy, the information would include: muscle origin; insertion; action; nerve supply; blood supply and diseases which can affect it. For pharmaceutics: name; minimum daily dose; signs of underdose and overdose, and so on. Myra would shuffle the cards, ask him the questions which were written on one side, and wait for the answer which should match that written on the obverse. If he 'got it right' the card would be placed in a 'yes' pile, if not, in a 'no' pile to be recycled. They would work thus through the entire day's material until there was nothing left in the 'no' pile, irrespective of how late that might be. This gave incentive, Geoff still declares, for him to learn and achieve so that they could both retire to 'what every young couple wants to do in bed'. Myra is not available to comment. Not far away, in Westley Street, East Hawthorn, lived Geoff's Aunt Cora,

Dot's, younger sister, known as 'Meg' and her husband Keith Hume-Cooke.

The couple's next home was in Tivoli Place, South Yarra, near the top of the Punt Road Hill up from the Yarra River Bridge. Here they rented digs in what had been RAF headquarters during the war. They had a rather dingy room in the basement of the building and were regularly disturbed during the night by the other occupants – a bunch of telephonists who noisily supplemented their income by nocturnal prostitution. On going to the toilet in the middle of the night, our friends would encounter all sorts of odd men in various stages of undress, roaming around the premises. On occasion Geoff was asked questions such as: 'How d' ya get out of here, mate?'

A time came when the landlord wished to move Geoff and Myra to an even more miserable part of the building. Uncle Keith inspected the premises – which were appalling, and insisted that they move to his mother's recently vacated house in Brighton. The widow had gone to Queensland for a time and needed someone to stay in her beautiful, Manor Street mansion which was close to the beach and to the Dendy Street shops. Myra and Geoff enthusiastically and gratefully accepted. 'The lovely old home was just a luxury. There was a little window called a servery, which you pulled up in the kitchen, to pass the dinner into the dining room.' Mr Shepherd, inventor of the 'Shepherd Castor' and his wife were their neighbours.

A few weeks before university resumed Geoff and Myra went to the seaside resort of Lorne on the Great Ocean Road, for a holiday. It was one of Victoria's most popular holiday venues situated on the south western coast, famous for its surf.

They booked into a 'private hotel' not knowing that this designation indicated that the premises – the Quamby Hotel – did not hold a liquor licence. The Misses Quamby ran a delightful establishment, 'so prim and proper it wasn't true', where the couple took a double room for two weeks. Myra and Geoff would sojourn to the local pub at night for dinner and a few drinks. Lorne was unlike anywhere either of them had ever known – 'a pretty freewheeling place', a mixture of fashion and bohemia, and they loved it. There they made friends with Ann and Graham Robertson, who:

> Were complete teetotallers but they'd come along to the pub with us. They lived at Caulfield with Ann's mother; Graham did all the painting, all the gardening. He had a tip truck business and later I would go with him to the hills at weekends and we'd load up firewood, saw it into lengths and go round and sell it to earn money to keep the budget going. That was our only income, apart from the bit I'd saved from war service days.

Eventually the Brighton home in which they were living was to be sold. Geoff and Myra needed to move house, yet again. Keith and Meg came to the rescue as before, introducing them to their friend Muriel Norwood, a lovely retired nurse who lived in an old house in the swanky suburb of Toorak. She'd moved into the household years before to look after the elderly and ailing Bert Brown. His wealthy family had owned the Mutual Store in Flinders Street in the City. When Bertie died he left his whole estate to Muriel.

Myra and Geoff moved in with Muriel to the deteriorated old gas lit house in Mathoura Road, right in the middle of the famous and very expensive 'Toorak Village'.

Geoff was delighted when the couple finally found a specialist, Mr Russell Buchanan, who believed that they could have children – one or perhaps even two – as long as Myra's heart condition was satisfactorily supervised. They had a happy time sharing the house with Muriel and it was here that Myra became pregnant with the couple's first child. Muriel had no relatives other than a nephew, who in turn later inherited her estate.

At weekends Myra and Geoff sometimes took the tram to Caulfield, to visit Ann and Graham Robertson whom they had met at Lorne. The Robertsons continued to live with Ann's mother, now with their two young daughters, Lynette and Joan as well.

The post war years were met with extraordinary flexibility by The University of Melbourne. The Faculty of Medicine intake quota was expanded to accommodate anyone who qualified academically for entrance, resulting in a first year group of some 180, in contrast to the traditional fifty-odd. The temporary expansion necessitated the recruitment of vast numbers of extra tutors in the subjects of Medicine and Surgery, so that the students could receive the required quality of input and supervision.

In the years after the war most of the lecturers were veterans, and had been doctors before the war. Many had also been POWs, although they were much older than Geoff and had served in different theatres of war. Geoff was allocated to a surgical tutor, Sir Edward 'Weary' Dunlop, who also lived in the Toorak area. Dunlop had served in the Middle East, Java and Thailand.

Weary noticed that Geoff was older than the other students and on learning why, was interested to hear more about his war experiences. Geoff declares that Weary's 'eyes lit up' at the prospect of mutual war stories. When a quick calculation revealed that Geoff had been a POW for longer than had Weary, the latter was impressed. After one of the lectures, Weary declared that Geoff should bring his wife 'around for dinner'.

Helen, Weary's wife and Myra quickly found that they were each at about the same stage of pregnancy. The men went off to talk war, and the women compared notes on their impending motherhood.

The couple had decided that Muriel Norwood, with whom they were still living, would be their baby's godmother. One day when Muriel and Myra were at the Prahran Market, Myra started to feel contractions. 'Out of here, quick!' exclaimed Muriel, 'no godchild of mine's going to be born in the fish market!' Myra had a quick labour giving birth to Adele, however her first words to her husband, from an ether-induced fog, were: 'If I ever see that thing again I'll cut it off'.

Eventually the Mathoura Road property was to be sold. Keith and Meg Hume Cooke (Geoff's aunt and her husband) invited the couple to share the Westley Street house with them, which they did. At this house the couple occupied a front room and Myra and Meg became good friends.

17

A REAL DOCTOR

Keith Hume Cooke had inherited money from his father and was keen to build a house at Croydon, 30 kilometres east of Melbourne. He had a block of land on Dorset Road, close to the house in which Ethel Turner had written her famous books including *Seven Little Australians*. An architect mate Andy, from Keith's days as a 'ground wallah' in the RAAF, designed the dwelling. Geoff willingly agreed to work as a builder's labourer on Keith's house. An incentive was that once Keith and Meg could move to Croydon, Geoff and Myra would have the house at 3 Westley Street, to themselves. Until now, the couple were almost always on the move. A period of stability followed and they stayed at Westley Street until after Geoff's medical course was completed.

Keith's job in RAAF disposals exposed him to some unusual bargains. He bought for relocation – actually for the timber, an old theatre building from Bairnsdale RAAF Base. Keith, Geoff and Keith's builder friend – 'fat little' Les, passed their weekends at Bairnsdale, staying in the Turf Club Hotel, by day dismantling the building at the old aerodrome and finally loading it onto semitrailers to be carried to Croydon. It was delivered to a double block adjacent to Croydon Railway Station where it was to be denailed, selected for use and stored. Keith planned to use the timber for his house, and Les already had a contract to build an RSL Hall opposite the station.

Once Geoff's work for Keith commenced he was able to catch the train to Croydon each day. His job was to pull out the old nails, sort the timber into categories, and set up storage to ensure that the materials would be protected from damage or deterioration. He was also employed by Les on the RSL project. Here he worked alongside and was more or less supervised by, an old communist – Darby Smith. Darby was middle aged, had eight children, been a builder's labourer all his life and rode to work on a bike. He was passionate about communism:

> He'd give me instructions how to dig, how to build the septic pit. It was deep clay, he'd put me at the bottom of the pit, in the clay with all the water. I'd throw it to a stage about four or five feet higher up. It would take twice as long to get my mud up to his level from where I was, as it took him to throw it out of the pit.
>
> He'd stop and roll a cigarette and lecture me about the virtues of communism. I argued with him about communism, and told him what I'd seen – you've never seen communism in action like I have, about how they didn't ever share anything. 'If we managed to throw a half a loaf of bread to the Russians, they'd just about kill each other to get at it – there was no sharing.' I'd fill him up with these stories of what I'd seen that'd shut him up for a while.

Geoff recalls that 'Les reckoned he never got as much work out of two blokes as he did out of us!' The work kept him fit and paid well. He admits to this day that Darby was good humoured, but that: 'I wasn't going to let him get away with extolling the virtues of communism to me!'

While Geoff was working at Croydon, the Transport Unions were alive and well and regularly calling strikes which affected both trams and trains, Geoff's principal modes of travelling to Croydon. Not to be daunted, Geoff simply rode his bicycle.

The government had paid for the first three years of Geoff's university training but the last three were a repayable loan. Even when Commonwealth Scholarships were established, these medical students were not able to transfer. 'We were silly enough to put up with that. We made a bit of a protest but nowadays of course we'd have put a bomb under Parliament House. We had to work so hard to pay back those fees.'

Geoff continued to study early in the morning and again at night so that he never wasted any time. Doing this all week left him free for the family at the weekends 'I tried to keep all the weekends free'.

Ann Robertson's mother developed dementia and she and Graham really had to move from Caulfield. They moved into Westley Street with Myra and Geoff. They spent a couple of congenial years sharing the house and when the Cornish family moved out the Robertsons stayed on and had the house to themselves.

As Geoff moved into final year the couple found they were expecting another child, this time unplanned. Myra's health had continued to deteriorate and even before the pregnancy it was evident she was very weak. She survived the pregnancy and a second daughter Sue, was born on 24 April 1951. Myra needed enormous amounts of sleep and had no energy reserves at all. She would go to bed early, Geoff would stay up to study and put Sue to the breast without waking his wife, then change the baby and go to bed himself. He would wake early and again put the baby to her mother's breast while Myra continued to sleep. Geoff was firmly of the view that babies should be fed on demand except for one feed per day – so they would learn a routine that suits the parents – and for his family that was to be the 6 am feed. 'I said, "We've got to set her clock because . . . the little buggers can sleep on and then when they wake they'd want to be fed".' He would then put the baby in her pram and have a shower himself by which time Myra would be awake. They'd have breakfast and Geoff would leave for university. Generally the baby slept through the night. It was very busy but that was the way life was.

On Saturdays there were lectures in the mornings after which the other students would go off to sport and Geoff would race home to have some time with the family. Towards the end of final year medicine Geoff knew what he would have liked to do:

> What I would love to have done was to specialise in paediatrics. I adored kids. They're such wonderful patients, you never get any hypochondriacs. When they're sick they're bloody sick when they're not sick they're outside playing. You'd do a house call and go into the bedroom – where is the little bugger – he's gone! Sure enough, she'd be apologetic. 'Look, it's alright, I came to help him. If he's alright already, that's fine. I'm not looking for work.' I still do like kids.

They managed that difficult year and Geoff passed his final exams. However, financially there was no possibility of his undertaking a specialisation.

As a graduate, he quickly obtained a short term position assisting in a general practice at Thornbury. Specialist Dr George Bearham maintained the general practice by employing two assistants and coming in a few half days himself. He had consulting rooms in Collins Street, lectured in Obstetrics and Gynaecology at the Royal Women's Hospital and consulted at the Freemasons' Hospital in East Melbourne. Geoff spent three months with that practice and Dr Bearham provided him with a Morris car, which was great. It made it easy to travel to and from work and he could take Myra and the girls out at the weekends.

In the meantime he was looking out for a permanent position and decided to apply for one in Tasmania. In early 1952 he moved to the position at Bronte Park, a town created for 2000 people, by the Tasmanian Hydroelectric Commission. The population comprised workers for the Scheme and their families, and the position offered quite a good salary, a small hospital, nurses, and an early model Holden car. The town, prefabricated elsewhere, had been towed up on huge trucks built specifically for hydroelectric work and the main power station was further up the hill. It was a solo practice which suited Geoff well because his experience in POW camps had given him plenty of practical experience, both in practical medicine and in working alone. He had performed well whilst doing his student time in Casualty.

The whole experience was a huge adventure and the family moved to Tasmania with much excitement and a little sadness, at leaving the friends they had made in Melbourne. Sue was about to have her first birthday.

Bronte Park was located in the very centre of Tasmania and was snow-covered in winter. The family were to live in married quarters in the village. In terms of human life, the hydroelectric scheme was a relatively high risk industry, owing to its geographical isolation combined with its rate of industrial and heavy vehicle accidents. The scheme was substantially staffed by young European men who had been living in displaced persons' camps after the war and had applied for immigration to Australia. Such immigrants were contracted to stay in Australia for a minimum of two years and during that time must work wherever the Australian government chose to put them. At Bronte Park, the men were housed in quarters separated by a major road from the town itself. During the late 1940s and '50s, these immigrants were the backbone of many Australian industries.

There was an average fatality rate of one death per 1.6 km of construction on the Hydro Scheme and the distance and accessibility of the major cities made it obvious to the young doctor that the lack of a supply of blood for emergency transfusions would be a problem. He quickly moved to rectify the problem by requesting a locally based small Red Cross Blood Bank be provided from Hobart. The Hobart central agency declined his request. Not to be deterred, Geoff proposed the establishment of a blood bank or collection centre locally. He and appropriate staff would regularly take blood from those willing to donate, amongst the huge number of fit, young men on the Scheme. After much disagreement and negotiation a local blood collection centre was established.

The mandatory requirements included: a comfortable area for donors; someone to stir the blood; sterile conditions; refrigeration large enough to hold 60–70 pint-bottles; perfect records; nursing staff; theatre technicians; a roll of donors; capacity to correctly screen the donors; someone capable of cross matching and typing the blood. Undaunted, Geoff returned to the town and called a public meeting which was well attended. There were five registered nurses living in the married quarters with their husbands who were amongst the professional workforce. It was proposed that the service be established. The Country Women's Association (CWA) found the necessary mattresses and blankets, the carpenters built trestle tables and the Freemasons donated a refrigerator which cost some 750 pounds ($1500). The blood collection occurred once a fortnight on Tuesday evenings, in a spare area of the hospital. Blood has a shelf life of three weeks when properly refrigerated, so at the end of each fortnight the surplus would be packed in ice and sent to Hobart for use there. Geoff says: 'We saved a local life three times and Hobart got 30 pints of fresh blood, twice per month, for nothing.'

Geoff went to the Hydro Scheme administration for help in finding someone suitable to train to assist with the blood typing. They searched their records and found one man whose former occupation had been 'medical student'. Klaus Gottschalk was a recently arrived German immigrant who had begun on the Scheme wielding a pick and shovel and progressed to working a jackhammer, which jobs paid excellent money for shifts and overtime. The scheme under which he had come to Australia was not government subsidised so he was paying back £2/14/6 ($6.45) per fortnight to the Australian Government. He was interviewed and appointed. 'Klaus, that's Nicholas in English. Can I call you Nick?' Geoff proffered. Arrangements were set up for 'Nick' to undertake instruction at the Royal Hobart Hospital, to qualify him to the standard required for the blood typing. Everything proceeded.

The blood collection scheme directly recruited donors from the fit young 'New Australian' men, through the Hydro Scheme's personnel officer. The men were keen to enjoy the personal attention and refreshments provided by the attractive young women who had volunteered to help. They 'processed' three donors at a time, 30 per session. Geoff describes the operation:

> Ten pretty girls did the stirring.[sic] Sisters scrubbed up and sterilised the equipment and area the previous evening and sealed everything with wax, the CWA did the supper and the school principal and two girls did all the recordkeeping. The men enjoyed the experience so much that many would try to come every fortnight! This was the first Red Cross blood collection centre to be established outside a capital city.

Geoff offered to coach Nick in English in return for his returning the favour with German lessons. Thus began another lifelong friendship. Nick recalls: 'I soon met Myra and the little girls, which led to an active social life. Sunday night was sacred: everyone listened to *The Goon Show* and had supper'. One can only surmise what the Goons must have done for the embryonic English of the new arrival. Nick also listened to *English for New Australians* daily, on ABC radio.

While located at Bronte Park Geoff went fortnightly to Hobart to do a ward round at the hospital. On these occasions once he and Myra knew Nick well, they engaged him to babysit their daughters, which he was very happy to do. This brought the ire of the engineer in charge of the camp. 'You are not to have a 'New Australian' in your home, in married quarters!' He bellowed. 'I'm not under your control and I'll do what I wish, I'll have anyone I choose,' Geoff shouted back.

'He was a pig of a man,' Geoff says now. 'His wife couldn't even wear makeup, no one ever denied him.'

Orry Fruehoff was another friend the family made whilst in Tasmania. Orry undertook all the really dangerous work around the Scheme, such as retrieving undischarged dynamite, because it attracted such enormous rates of pay. He would simply walk into the pit or whatever, apparently quite unafraid. He later performed the same function on the Snowy Mountains Scheme which enabled him to buy land at Falls Creek in the Victorian Alps where he built the fashionable *Winterhaven* Ski Lodge. Years later, Geoff and his elder daughter Adele would visit *Winterhaven* as Orry's guests in winter and Sue and her mother in summer. Myra had 'seen enough snow' to last her a lifetime and would only visit during the milder season.

While at Bronte Park Geoff was visited by a now famous friend from his university days in Perth. Shirley Strickland's brother Ron came to work on the Scheme and quickly found Geoff and Myra – the Western Australians sought each other out in the same manner as did the various European groups. Shirley had won Gold at the 1952 Helsinki Olympic Games and wished to visit her brother. She was of course not allowed to stay in the single men's quarters with him, so she stayed with the Cornish family and had great fun with the little girls and Myra. In all, Shirley won Gold at three consecutive Olympic Games.

The time at Bronte Park was happy and challenging for Geoff: 'All our age, all young marrieds with kids so you got to know them. You got to know everyone. I immunized all the kids. It was a joy for me to work there but very lonely for Myra because it was not easy for her to get out.' After about a year, when Geoff was starting to think about moving on, his former lecturer and tutor, Sir Edward 'Billy' Hughes came through central Tasmania on his way to Hobart and Launceston. Bronte was on the road between the two cities so Sir Edward and his wife Alison visited the family. Hughes performed surgery at Warrugul Hospital in Gippsland, Victoria, in conjunction with the local GP at Drouin. At the time the Drouin practice was seeking an assistant and it was suggested that Geoff go and investigate. Hughes loaned him a car and he and Myra drove to Drouin. The little Renault hummed along like a ladybird. Geoff was offered and accepted the position. The family left Bronte Park in March 1953, not realising that Hughes had really set it up, because he recognised that Tasmania was just too isolated for them.

18

To the mainland

Geoff stayed nearly three years as Assistant at the Drouin practice, which covered a large area and grew quickly with the extra practitioner. Again a supply of blood was a problem. Again Geoff tackled it, with the result that in 1954 a 'remote' blood collection base was established, this time at the regional West Gippsland Hospital in Warragul. Donors came from Drouin, Neerim, and Yarram in community buses. That regional blood bank became the model for a total of fifty eight rural blood banks by 1988. The Hospital had closed its pathology department because it could not obtain staff. This concerned Geoff greatly and he suggested that he might be able to recruit someone to fill the post. He brought Nick Gottschalk from Tasmania to take up the position and had him attend the Royal Melbourne Hospital (as WGHs employee) for six months to gain practical experience while he attended lectures at Melbourne University. This worked well and Nick remained at the hospital for many years. Geoff did a little matchmaking on the side which resulted in Nick marrying Helen, a nurse at the hospital, in 1957, with Geoff, unsurprisingly, performing the function of best man.

His interest in anaesthetics – in those days closely related to his long-love, resuscitation, grew rapidly. He removed the back seat of his Volkswagen 'beetle' and stored his resuscitation equipment there on a permanent basis. This enabled him to service surgeries all across the region including many dentists, who had previously always admitted their patients to hospital when an anaesthetic was required.

Early in Geoff's time at Drouin his boss told him that a local Rotary Group was being set up, but that he was not planning to join because it would eat into his time in the practice. Later Geoff was approached to join and agreed, to the obvious annoyance of his colleague who could not envisage a financial return from the activity. Rotary International would become a major interest for Geoff for the rest of his life.

Geoff was amused at some of the economy measures in the practice, which were probably derived from experience of the Depression. When the mail arrived, the envelopes would be opened very carefully – then cut so that the front could be used as a prescription form: 'why have them printed specially when they arrive free every day?' It was legal, but frugal. When a certificate was to be issued for a patient on Worker's Compensation, it was not permissible to give it to the patient, so it was mailed in an unsealed envelope, which cost a half-penny less to post than did a sealed letter. Letters to Consultants were sent in sealed envelopes and all the stamps were carefully accounted for every week. Geoff purchased the ha'penny stamps himself, to allow his mail to be sealed.

While he was at this practice, Geoff's boss guaranteed him an overdraft to enable him to buy a house, for which he says he may have paid too much money, but at least secured the family a home. The house was on one a third of an acre, a generous block, but turned out to be full of borers.

Myra was homesick for England and her father was ill, so Geoff agreed that she and the girls could go there and stay for up to a year. While they were away he worked on the house. He climbed into the roof with a syringe and squirted poison into all the holes. He painted the house inside and out and borrowed a rotary hoe from a friend to improve the block and the garden. The beautiful red soil responded well to care, and when Myra, Adele and Sue returned, the whole place was a picture. Adele started preschool in England and the two girls had a lot of fun with their British relatives.

By late 1955, aged thirty four, Geoff decided that it was time to move on again. He investigated the possibility of joining a practice at Frankston, a major centre closer to Melbourne. He wanted to go but when he told his boss, the reaction was not good. 'You can't!' his employer ordered. 'I can, I've cleared the overdraft,' Geoff responded. In addition, the family made a profit of more than a thousand pounds on selling the first house, a goodly sum in those days. Geoff had by now gained a lot of anaesthetic experience, including having serviced the practice that he was now about to join. The senior partner, John Ackroyd, son of a former governor of Pentridge Prison, was a prominent local citizen and a member of all the local institutions. He was Geoff's first real business partner.

Commencing in December 1955, Geoff was happy to follow whatever specialisation his colleagues wished. They discussed which niche he might fill. All were general practitioners, each with a special interest, and Geoff now had four years' general practice experience. 'What do you want me to do?' he asked with no particular inclination. 'Continue with anaesthesia,' was the reply. So he did and eventually made it his specialisation.

Geoff soon learned that Ackroyd was well connected with his longstanding hero, 'Weary' Dunlop. The pair had gone through kindergarten, primary school, secondary school, and university together in the same class, were great mates, played rugby together, and were captured together. While they were prisoners of war, John as a physician was kept in the camp at Changi, while Weary, a surgeon, was on the move to the

Burma-Thai Railway and elsewhere. After the war John resumed practice in Frankston, having maintained it with locums in the interim. On alternate Saturday mornings Weary would come to operate at Frankston Hospital on complicated cases, and Geoff assisted as anaesthetist. Although he was routinely only rostered one Saturday in five, when Weary came he would always attend. When the men finished the operating list, usually around lunchtime, they would sojourn to the Frankston RSL for lunch. John, a Life Member, had been Branch President since the end of the war, ruling that roost as if it were itself a military organisation! It was run well, but not to the taste, by then, of the majority of members. Ackroyd and Dunlop were both 120 kilos and Geoff around 60, so he had no hope of matching their drinking capacity.

Although Geoff bought his rounds of drinks, half of his beer went into the closest potted palms. 'I knew that I would slip away into a beautiful stupor after about three drinks'. He would take his leave while still in reasonable shape, but really enjoyed the fun and the company. Sometimes they would proceed to Mornington, to the little bush nursing hospital where Geoff would again administer the anaesthetics. On those occasions they forewent the drinks.

On joining the Frankston practice Geoff moved into a house owned by Ackroyd at Seaford. During the six months prior to becoming a partner, he painted the house with materials provided by Ackroyd. He became involved in discussion with a German patient, who with her husband operated a 'barbecued chicken' roadhouse between Gippsland and Frankston, which premises Geoff recalls his daughters could sense, even if they were asleep, a mile away. On approaching the shop during the Drouin days, when the family was driving citywards or home, the girls would wake, sit bolt upright, and demand a 'cooked chook.' The proprietors had another business, the confectionery stall at the Frankston cinema and were planning to sell their farm at Cranbourne Road, Langwarrin, 6 km out of Frankston. It was on 45 acres of land, near Union Road and Dame Elisabeth Murdoch's *Cruden Farm*. Geoff bought the property and the family lived there for six years.

At Frankston Geoff repeated his by now regular practice of attempting to set up a blood service. Again, the central authority refused his request on the basis that the area was too large, but offered to send the mobile blood bank once a week. Geoff became the 'Regional Director of Blood Transfusion Services' a high sounding title for a relatively small part of his workload, but enjoyable work nonetheless, and a satisfactory outcome in ensuring a locally available blood supply. After three years in the Frankston practice anaesthesia was proving to be a very large responsibility.

Geoff arranged to spend Wednesday afternoons working alongside Sir Benjamin Rank at the plastics surgery unit at The Royal Melbourne Hospital. He hoped to complete a post-graduate qualification in anaesthesia whilst with Sir Benjamin but pressure of work at the Frankston practice rendered that impossible. By 1960 he had decided that he would continue to specialise in anaesthetics. Demand in the provincial area was enormous, and he was continually mindful that at any time he could need to resuscitate his increasingly frail wife.

Relatively early in the family's time at Frankston and on the farm, in 1957 when aged thirty four, Myra required her first heart operation. With two heart valves linked, stiffened and failing, and knowing that no one with her condition had passed their thirty-fifth birthday, her increasing weakness was a serious issue for the whole family. She was technically in heart failure and approaching death. A British cardiac specialist, Sir Russell Brock, visited Melbourne at this time, lecturing on the newest techniques and successes. He assessed Myra and decreed that she was an ideal case and could be done immediately.

Things went well. Geoff's motivation to rehabilitate his wife could not have been higher. He walked with her slowly every day in the coronary care unit, a practice that was unusual in the days when patients were kept bed-bound after surgery and consequently often developed complications that are now a thing of the past. Her pace slowly increased day by day, round and round the corridors of the unit, further and further, faster and faster. Geoff tells us that Myra broke the recovery records for rehabilitation. Her health took a leap forward and it was a full fourteen years before her own valves were so worn that they required replacement with artificial ones. On the second occasion, a similar rehabilitation regime was followed.

Soon after this the National Heart Foundation began regional programmes, and sought regionally based practitioners who would be willing to participate. Geoff designed a programme for the Foundation, based on Myra's recovery. He contributed one half day per week to that project, which he was determined to see succeed. 'I'll make it work,' he vowed. 'I did. I got such a wonderful kick out of it. Most of the patients had virtually given up, and when they started to improve it was very satisfying.'

'In anaesthetics,' he explains, 'there is virtually no doctor-patient relationship. "Hello Paul, I'm Geoff Cornish. Count to ten, please" and they're out on seven or eight, and that is the end of your meeting with them.'

With his new programme, Geoff had his charges walking every morning at a pace which he would set for each of them individually. He could watch them regaining their optimism and confidence, gradually realising that they could become as fit again as they had been years before. Geoff ran the programme for some years with the support of the local Council and other professionals.

Once the family were living on the farm life was stable for some six years. The girls went to St Paul's Primary School in Frankston, Adele for her last four years (she had already attended Drouin and Langwarrin) and Sue for six full years. Adele attended boarding secondary school at St Margaret's, Berwick for a year, which she had begged to do. However she was so homesick she would come home sobbing at the weekends. Sue's whole six secondary years were spent at Toorak College, Mount Eliza where Adele joined her for the rest of her secondary education.

Farm life suited them all, despite Geoff's working life always going at a frenetic pace. He worked long hours as a GP and later, when running his own anaesthetic practice he could be on call seven days per week, twenty four hours a day.

Myra had spent some years during the war living with relatives in a hotel in Wales. Not only did this hone her singing and socialisation skills, but she also learnt quite a lot about antique furniture. She had first started going to auctions – Leonard Joel, Aingers and the like – from Westley Street. When living on the farm she established an antique business in Frankston Arcade. She named the shop *Glenfern Antiques* after the Mathoura Road house, from which she had made her first antique investment purchases so many years before. She bought goods from the scrap metal yard in Wells Road Frankston – beautiful old lamps, chairs and a mosaic frame which Adele still treasures. The man would rush out to meet her 'Hello Mrs Cornish!' They went to a clearing sale at the farm owned by Neville Shute, the author of the novel *On the Beach*. She sent home container loads of antiques when she went to England. The television celebrity Graham Kennedy was a 'regular' at the shop and visited the family at the farm, 'a lovely man' who made regular purchases. Geoff was also active in the business during his small amounts of spare time. He turned an area at the back of the shop into a little coffee area, with Persian rugs hanging on the walls from hooks and pulleys. All sorts of friends and customers would call in for a coffee when in town. Geoff had a roof rack on the same VW which had his anaesthetic equipment in the back, and would stop and collect things for the shop as he travelled around.

In 1960 Geoff decided to leave the medical group and develop his own business. He set up in Beach Street, Frankston and took a partner, Barry McKean. McKean then bought the General Practice from Geoff and Geoff moved into fulltime anaesthesia, from the same rooms, which they continued to share. Building upon the mobile resuscitation system which he had developed at Drouin, Geoff constructed a fully equipped mobile anaesthetic department in a van. He employed a specialist sister and in conjunction with Commonwealth Industrial Gasses (CIG), installed a full, 'state of the art', miniaturised Boyle's anaesthetic machine. Against warnings that he would be broke within months, the business flourished, providing on call service twenty four hours a day, seven days a week. The practice serviced an area from Frankston to Warragul, where the many small bush nursing hospitals really had no anaesthetic provision at all.

After a short while a second practitioner was required and extensive advertising attracted a doctor from Britain. Geoff had to guarantee Mike Mantell's employment, and provide him a house and car to satisfy the immigration and sponsorship requirements. This he did and the practice continued to flourish and grow. Eventually more assistance was required and further wide advertising took place. Three good applicants were identified. They employed all three and the practice continued to expand. Eventually there were some eighteen anaesthetists working between Dandenong and Frankston and the group had established the region's first day surgery in David Street, Dandenong, next to the hospital. The duty doctor would sleep there at night in order to be immediately available.

In 1962 Geoff took a trip to Perth with his brother Roy to attend the Commonwealth Games. After three weeks the family had not heard a word from him and his angry wife wrote 'Have you broken both your arms?' 'He tends not to communicate with family,' his daughter Sue says, 'that's just the way he is.' She finishes fondly: 'I have a rapport with him.'

'Never marry a doctor, Suzie,' Myra would say so many times to her daughter. Sue has a permanent memory of a plate on top of a saucepan keeping her father's dinner warm. Geoff loved life on the farm, the realisation of a dream since visiting his Auntie Gwen and Uncle Syd all those years before. The family had dairy cattle, horses, the odd sheep – old ewes which were ready for the slaughter yard – and chickens. On one occasion they fattened piglets for Christmas.

Geoff's daughters Adele and Sue relate more detailed memories of the farm than does their father. Sue recalls:

> It was a lovely place to grow up. We had lots of birthday parties and all the kids could come and stay, ride the horses and everything. We had huge bonfire nights, although Mum wouldn't do fireworks – they reminded her of the bombings during the war.
>
> Mum loved having visitors, she would spend days cooking, she was very vivacious, a great entertainer. Scones and jersey cream. We'd have everyone come down to stay.

Adele tells the story of the time Myra prepared breakfast for Geoff, a rare event. 'Sorry darling, I'm in a hurry.' 'You'll have it anyway,' Myra retorted and accurately landed the bacon and eggs on the middle of the back of his suit coat as he reached the door.

All of the family helped with the milking but Sue has two particular stories about her mother. On one occasion, Geoff and Myra were going to a ball and Geoff phoned to say he would be late: 'Could you do the milking please?' Myra obliged, staying in her balldress and simply adding gumboots. The other occasion was the time when Myra had finished milking and could not get the cow to move despite repeated 'shooing'. She eventually discovered that she still had its tail tied to the stall. On another occasion she filled her boots with milk. The dairy business was reasonably successful and their 'Pine Ranch' cream was a local delicacy.

Geoff liked to fatten up animals for slaughter. He sometimes did his own slaughtering of the old ewes for pet food ('I had a terrific recipe!') and gave Sue an anatomy lesson while he was cutting them up. He would repeat the performance while carving the Sunday roast.

The farm also had poultry but his daughter reports that Geoff was not prepared to do anything more with the chooks than the killing. Myra 'had to sit outside and pluck and clean them'. Geoff's defence is that the first time he killed a chicken, his wife *insisted* that she would pluck it, that she knew what to do, and did not require any instruction. Geoff returned to find her pulling the feathers out of the dry carcass, with great difficulty and much swearing. 'There were feathers flying and dogs everywhere!' Another livestock venture was the pigs. A couple of piglets were purchased to be fattened for Christmas. Sue remembers them being 'delightful pets' especially the time when afternoon tea guests were being entertained and the piglets invited themselves inside, trotting straight into the sitting room to the guests, skidding across the beautifully polished jarrah floor. The piglets were finally taken to Lloyd's [abattoir] to be slaughtered and hung. After that, the meat had to hang again at home. They were wrapped to protect them from flies, but unfortunately in plastic. 'I don't know what Dad could have been thinking of,' Sue declares. The meat rapidly rotted in the heat, hanging on the clothesline in the plastic bags. The Christmas delicacy came to naught and the girls had lost their lovely pets.

Another hobby of the family and Myra in particular was the breeding and showing of Boxer dogs. The dogs had a number of litters from which the girls were sometimes allowed to keep one puppy. One went to the home of actors John MacCallum and Googie Withers. When the Cornishes old friends Helen and Nick Gottschalk had their first son, Myra presented them with a puppy – which proceeded to tear the baby's nappies from the clothesline. A novel 'baby gift' to say the least.

Snakes were often seen on the farm, especially in summer. On one occasion while Sue was at home studying, the dogs started barking furiously and she found a huge tiger snake rearing up on the front drive. She phoned a family friend who drove straight round and narrowly missed hitting it with the car. They would put a saucer outside with a broken egg in it to attract the snakes and make them easier to catch and kill. They would then hang the carcases in the trees, as trophies.

The farm had a large area of tea tree which, by arrangement, neighbours were permitted to cut for fencing. On one occasion Myra saw some unexpected intruders entering the property and followed them with the loaded .22 rifle. It turned out that they had come to harvest tea tree for fencing but no one knew that they were coming. Sue recalls 'Mum – all five feet of her – with the shotgun bigger than herself, took off in the car down to the paddock after them'. A fiery Welsh temperament and a shotgun could have been a force to be reckoned with.

Myra's mother, Win came from England to stay with the family at the farm as she had done many years before at Hawthorn. This time she earned her return fare by working for Geoff's practice, sterilising the syringes and sharpening the needles. The girls loved having their colourful Welsh grandmother to stay and enjoyed their time with her.

One school holidays, when Adele was about eight years old, she attended sewing classes in Frankston and quickly found her niche. She came home and paraded around with a tape around her neck like a 'real dressmaker' and immediately started designing. She subsequently decided to study fashion design at the Emily McPherson College in Melbourne. The vacation before Sue's last year of secondary school, her father suggested that she and a friend might like to do voluntary work with the physiotherapists at the Orthopaedic Hospital at Mt. Eliza where Geoff was the regular anaesthetist. The girls took up the offer and so much enjoyed their work with the multiply disabled children that they both made career decisions – Sue to study physiotherapy and her friend Gail, to become a teacher of children with a disability. 'Two careers in one week!' Geoff still declares proudly.

After Sue's Matriculation year the family took a trip on the Gippsland Lakes on a 'Bull's Cruiser' – a wonderful holiday, during which they chugged in to Paynesville for Sue to check her exam results, in those days only available through the metropolitan newspapers. This proved to be the only flaw in the holiday – Geoff grounded the dinghy in which they rowed to shore for the paper. Sue passed her examinations handsomely and gained a place in the physiotherapy course. 'She was in such floods of tears that she couldn't read the results herself,' Geoff says.

As Myra became more ill and the girls, now in their teens, required more and more chauffeuring around, it was time to move closer to town. The Cornishes formed a partnership – 'Pine Ranch Pastoral Company' with their friends Martin and Joan Keeley. The Keeley couple and their nine children moved onto the farm and the Cornish family moved to Cliff Road Frankston. In 1963 they sold the farm and Martin bought into a Frankston Volkswagen dealership.

Once the two girls were established in their tertiary study courses in Melbourne their parents thought that it was time for the family to live closer to the city. Geoff would now do the commuting. They rented a flat in Darling Street, South Yarra which was an easy bus or tram trip to the city for both daughters, and Geoff drove to Frankston against the traffic. During that year – 1969 – Geoff and Myra flew to Britain for the twenty-fifth anniversary of The Great Escape and Muriel Norwood moved into the flat with the girls while their parents were away.

The system worked quite well but after a year Myra and Geoff yearned to return to the peninsula. Adele and Sue were by now well established in the city, both were busy, happy and had made friends. The girls moved to a flat in Elsternwick and their parents moved to a rented a house near Frankston, at 3 Daveys Bay Road, Mount Eliza, just in time for Adele's twenty-first birthday party. The house became known as 3DB – the name of one of Melbourne's commercial radio stations. Geoff soon found a house to buy, a 'funny little fibro cottage', next to a nursery in Bembridge Avenue, at the top of Oliver's Hill, 'We just walked in and had to have it.' The house lent itself to extension, renovation and the addition of a swimming pool, and was a comfortable home for another six years.

It was at Bembridge Avenue, in 1971, that Myra had her stroke. Her health had been gradually deteriorating for a long time and she had been assessed for surgery. On Geoff's fiftieth birthday, Myra had been to hospital for tests and returned home. The testing must have dislodged a clot and she had a stroke the very same day, sitting in her chair while Geoff was carving the roast dinner. He phoned for an ambulance – 'there have to be some benefits of being the Director of Anaesthetics'. It came immediately and Myra was back at the Royal Melbourne in thirty minutes, with the ambulance being led by a Police escort. After a time in hospital Myra stabilised and returned home to build up her strength for the surgery which would become even more urgent as time went by.

In the garden there was a two-person swing, in which Myra would lie for hours on end in the sun. Typically she would sleep up to twenty three hours a day while recovering from the stroke. She recovered and had surgery the following year.

Prior to being admitted to hospital for the second operation, Myra went for a holiday to Tasmania, to stay with an old friend and relax. Whilst in Hobart she found a beautiful full length mink coat in one of the stores, which she decided, was just what she needed. She stepped off the 'plane wearing said garment and tried to calm her husband's financial shock by promising to pay for it out of the housekeeping money. 'What could I do?' Geoff pleads, when he tells the story.

After many arduous hours in theatre, and many more hours unconscious, while still surrounded by and filled with tubes, she signalled to her husband that she wanted a paper and pencil. She wrote 'How does the mink look now, darling?' Probably 'Much like the same overdraft that it had before'.

For a second time the couple made rehabilitation history.

Myra was much better straight after the operation but soon began to go downhill again.

As a result of or in reaction against, his experiences as a prisoner of war, Geoff operated the anaesthetic practice as a 'complete democracy'. Big mistake! Eventually the younger men wanted to change the system completely, to split the practice and have Geoff work in Dandenong – 'when Frankston was my home'. Generally life became unworkable. After some agony, he decided to bale out and return to solo practice. His daughters were now well off his hands and Myra was growing weaker by the day. He decided to recommence practice in the Warragul area and bought a farm at Jindivik, near the base of the Baw Baw plateau.

While at Jindivik Geoff went for a short time as a medical locum to Alice Springs. When he returned, Myra commented that he didn't have much of a suntan. 'That's something I tried to avoid,' he replied. Myra then noticed a mark on his back. On investigation it turned out to be a melanoma. He had it checked and found it to be malignant. He was the first patient on his colleagues' operating list the next Saturday. This was the first of a series of malignancies which Geoff attributes to his days in the sun and surf as a teenager, 'when nobody even knew about sun protection'.

Although working in Gippsland was enjoyable and the farm a pleasant environment, the climate was quite destructive to Myra's deteriorating health. One day when Geoff went into Bill Suhr, the dentist, Bill asked him to buy a raffle ticket. Geoff was happy to do so and gave the matter no more thought.

On his next visit he was told that he had won the raffle. 'What is it?' asked the lucky winner. 'A coach trip to the Gold Coast' was the reply, 'including accommodation.'

19

PARADISE FOUND

So Myra and Geoff set off for their holiday in 1981 and enjoyed the trip north immensely. 'We stayed one block away from Cavill Avenue in Surfers Paradise, at a little B&B where the Chateau is now. There was no restaurant but a beautiful little French Café just over the road.'

They stayed two weeks, right in the centre of the resort. A bonus was that at the time the couple's daughter Sue, with her husband and children, lived in Brisbane. It was a great prize. The warm climate agreed with Myra and they loved the fact that she didn't have to walk far, that they were 'right there where everything was happening' in central Surfers Paradise. Geoff adds:

> It was so cold at Jindivik. She did take a downturn. We discussed whether we might move north. When we went home I just said 'right', we'll go. Sue was up there, they lived at The Gap and she had the children. We came up again, because I didn't want to move and not already have somewhere to live. The minute Myra stepped off the plane she felt better.

The apartment block 'Benelong', at 1 Whelan Street was newly built, part sold, and the couple considered it absolutely beautiful. It faced north, straight up the Broadwater, with

Surfers Paradise to the right, and the Isle of Capri to the left. There was car parking; everything was brand new. No one had lived in the Unit which took Myra and Geoff's fancy, but they would have to take a lease from that very day if they wished it secured. They paid three months advance rent and returned to Victoria to settle their business and lives there. 'It'll be gone before you come back,' Geoff was told, so he faced a very expensive few months. On returning to Jindivik: 'I just sold up. I didn't care what I got.'

Surfers Paradise was just perfect for Myra. The climate provided benefits for her health and she would sleep late in the mornings while Geoff went downstairs to throw a fishing line into the adjacent Nerang River before leaving for work.

Geoff says that he would sometimes have three rods in three holders, and he claims that 'It was not unknown to have all three screaming at once with fish on them'. While living at Benelong they met the Ramsays. On first meeting his neighbour on the river bank, Geoff had no idea who the man was. One morning, the neighbour put his head over the fence and said 'Catching any fish?' Geoff showed him his bucket. 'Do you mind if I throw a line in?' his new acquaintance asked. The neighbour was the Governor of Queensland, Sir James Ramsay. That started a delightful friendship. 'He was so friendly, he was a West Australian and of course I didn't realise he was the governor then. They had the unit above us; it was their hideaway retreat. On Friday afternoon the Rolls would come down from Government House and a chauffeur would take all their luggage up to their unit.'

Geoff decided to make his hobby – cardiac rehabilitation – his future profession and reduced his work in anaesthetics accordingly. He adapted the walking programme which he had first developed for Myra into a full scale rehabilitation programme for use by residents of the Gold Coast.

He found consulting rooms in Nerang Street, Southport and commenced the cardiac practice. He transferred his Rotary membership from Gippsland to Southport, which provided him with at least one network of friends in his new location. He went to AMA meetings, but 'They must have thought that I was someone from the South with a lot of smart bloody ideas, and didn't want to know me'. For the first three months he received no referrals. Then Dr Cliff Wright, with whom Geoff had studied medicine in Melbourne, referred a colleague to him. Cliff was ex-navy, had lived on the Coast for many years and had a well-developed practice. The referred patient had 'A shocking heart, awful angina and he improved very quickly,' Geoff recalls, 'So Cliff sent a lot of patients after that'. Geoff continued practising anaesthesia while he built up his heart practice, again offering a mobile service to dental and medical practitioners. He anticipated that there would eventually be a good living to be made in his new specialty.

Myra's health continued to deteriorate, but Geoff says that she knew her limits and stayed within them. Shopping centres provided entertainment for her, with Pacific Fair having just opened and Sundale at Southport being more established. Pacific Fair had a lot of car space and three good little restaurants right down on the river's edge. The couple frequently ate out, which they both enjoyed. Myra resumed her hobbies of growing African violets and knitting sweaters for her family in the South. She had black wool sent up from Melbourne until a neighbour said: 'Goodness, we're throwing it out!' Their family had a property near Casino, which bred sheep and produced fine wool. They delivered Myra a whole bale of black wool, which the farm otherwise discarded. Another friend was a gem cutter. Myra had a little lathe for faceting stones, which motivated the couple to go fossicking at weekends. They bought emeralds from the permanent fossickers and Myra would polish them for gifts. She also took sewing lessons at a shop where the customer would select their material and pattern and be taught how to construct a garment. 'She was so chuffed with herself,' Geoff smiles.

Each year, during the hottest part of the Queensland summer, it was planned that Myra would go south to have her heart treatment reassessed. She would be admitted to the Royal Melbourne Hospital, undergo tests and have her medication reviewed. She would then spend a few days with daughter Adele and her family before returning home to Queensland. Her first such trip, in the summer of 1982 was successful but on the whole her condition continued to deteriorate. Otherwise life was stable.

In the summer of 1983 Myra and Geoff's granddaughter Amy had been holidaying with them. She was to return home to Melbourne by plane with her grandmother when Myra was to have her medical review at the Royal Melbourne Hospital. Geoff waved his wife and little granddaughter off at the airport.

Myra delivered Amy safely and stayed ten days in the Royal Melbourne. Her physician said that he would like to keep her there permanently: 'She's such a tonic to the people who are going in to have their ops done.' They were all so new and so terrified. 'What the hell are you worrying about' she would say, 'I've had two!' She would sit on the patients' beds and cheer them up. 'She does more for the patients than the nurses do!' he said laconically. Myra introduced the specialist to the woman who would become his wife.

Myra went to Adele's home to stay for a few days before returning to Queensland on the Sunday, Valentines Day. Geoff chatted by phone with Myra about her plane booking and how much he was looking forward to her return. Two hours later Adele rang and said 'Dad, Mum has just died'.

Myra had collapsed and Adele immediately phoned her mother's specialist. He was nearby and came quickly, but there was nothing he could do. Geoff was distraught. He went straight to Melbourne. He could never have dreamt that the last he might see of Myra alive, would be with her hand in Amy's as she went up the steps of their aeroplane. It was eleven years after her second operation and she was about to have her sixtieth birthday.

20

When I'm 64

After the saddest trip of his life, Geoff returned home: 'I had to come back quickly to the Coast; you can't just walk out of a practice you're trying to establish'.

Thus began a new life for Geoff and a period of painful adjustment. His mother Dot came from Perth to stay with him for a few months which offered him some stability in those difficult days.

'Thank God I had my practice. It kept me busy and occupied but there was nothing socially at all. I wasn't enjoying it one little bit, I grieved for a long time; I never expected to marry again.'

Alison Angus had retired from Sydney to the Gold Coast with her husband Bill, in 1981. Some time later, Bill had suffered a heart attack and died. Alison was also now alone. The relatively young widow tried various means of filling the space in her life but was quickly bored with the rounds of bowling and bridge. She had always been very physically active and yearned to become really fit again. Hearing about Dr Cornish's walking programme, she wondered if it might be good for her. 'Not for the likes of you, my dear' was the opinion of her local doctor. However, Alison was undeterred and eventually phoned

Dr Cornish directly. The sister asked how many heart attacks the prospective patient had experienced. 'We'll have to get you to come into the rooms for assessment.' Mrs Angus willingly agreed and an appointment was arranged.

The new patient kept her appointment and was assessed, passing the physical test with flying colours. 'I'm recently widowed,' she explained. 'I know all about that!' was the reply. The doctor said that he'd had plenty of widows on the programme. The interview continued rather longer than the usual medical assessment. The doctor told his new patient all about life down south and on his farm; she retaliated with her tales of life on the property on the Hawkesbury River. She learnt about his ability to construct animal sheds, manage cattle and generally juggle farm life with medical practice. Her tales of farm life kept pace with his.

'It was so different,' Geoff recalls. 'Alison came in and said she wanted to get fit. She mentioned that she'd not long lost her husband. So I did what she suggested, checked her out, she was just so vivacious and lovely and . . . friendly, really friendly.'

After some discussion it was agreed that Mrs Angus would join the walkers on the programme at 5.30 next morning. She attended regularly and quickly became fitter, whilst actively assisting others on the programme. She gained a new sense of purpose and the company and exercise she was seeking. She told Geoff that if there were any other ways that she could help him . . . Geoff continues:

> At that stage we'd got Council permission to mark out tracks along the Gold Coast Highway, a white mark with a red heart in the centre of it, along what had been the Gold Coast Marathon strip. It had to be done at the crack of dawn, because painting strips on the road with your backside up in

> the air . . . was difficult to do on your own, jumping in and out of the car, and pretty hazardous. I asked would she like to help me: 'I'd love to' was the reply.

Alison elaborates:

> 'Would it present any problems for you if I came around at 4.30?' he asked.
>
> 'None at all.'

The next morning before dawn, the doctor arrived, in his little old Suzuki with cans of paint and other paraphernalia in the back. 'I had to drive, while he bobbed in and out of the back of the car. It certainly could have been a hazard,' Alison says.

Geoff smiles: 'Alison well remembers one of our first dates being . . . Well, that was semi-business, really, but I thought "gosh she's nice". I soon asked her if she'd come out to dinner'.

Alison's phone rang: 'Geoff Cornish here. What sort of a day have you had?' Geoff himself had been busy. 'Would you like to come to see Goldie Hawn? A wacky blonde. She'll give you a good laugh.' Alison accepted and the couple had an early dinner at the classy Broadbeach restaurant 'Volare' before the film. During the show Alison turned to make a comment to Geoff and found him asleep.

The couple saw a good deal of each other over the ensuing weeks – walking, surfing and swimming, taking in films and live shows. They had many interests in common, similar life experiences and an uncanny number of mutual friends and connections. They spent many happy hours strolling the beaches along the coast. Alison was aware that Geoff loved children, and when he would see kiddies on the beach: 'He's just not there. You might as well go home; he'll be down on the sand, building castles with them.'

Alison's husband, Bill Angus had been a 'Rat of Tobruk'. He had signed up to war in May 1940, served with infantry in the Middle East, later returned to Australia and was then redeployed to New Guinea. He and Alison Keogh had met in October 1940, shortly after his twenty-first birthday. He left Brisbane on Christmas Day, 1940 to sail from Sydney on the Queen Mary, for Tobruk.

On Bill's return to Australia in March 1943 the couple announced their engagement, during his three weeks' leave before being sent to New Guinea, where a bullet destined for Captain Angus as leader, killed the man standing beside him.

Some time later Alison's phone rang: 'I'll see you tomorrow; I'll come in to the bank.' It was Bill, en route to Southport to undertake commando training, after which he applied for leave and the couple were married. They departed by train to honeymoon at Narrowneck on the south coast.

The next day they visited the beach soon after dawn. Bill fell into the surf and was unable to stand. His malaria, contracted in the tropics, had returned. After much reorganisation, Bill spent his honeymoon leave in Greenslopes Hospital with his new wife visiting daily.

All too soon Captain Angus returned to service, but not too much later was relocated back to Atherton. Alison requested a bank posting to Atherton to be near her husband. It was granted. While living at Ravenshoe, Alison learned that she was pregnant. Suzanne, the couple's first child was born in Brisbane in March 1945. The war ended in October that year. Bill's parents were opposed to their son marrying a Catholic and for many years the couple saw little of them, which Alison says had a significant effect on their lives. Their sons Ian and Terry were born in 1946 and 1950 respectively.

On retiring, they moved from Sydney to their former hobby farm on the Hawkesbury River. They had a very happy four years at the farm but eventually Bill's heart problems forced them to leave. He had had a number of cardiac arrests, from one of which Alison had resuscitated him single handedly while awaiting the arrival of an ambulance. In 1981 they moved to the Gold Coast. He died there in 1983.

Geoff Cornish tells us what he learned about Alison's husband, Bill Angus:

> His citation for the Military Cross. When we were engaged, just getting married and sorting things out, she was going through papers and she gave me this citation for his Military Cross. Gosh, it makes the hair stand up on the back of your neck, what he did. Basically, he was in charge of a patrol and they saw some Germans in front of them, at night. One of the guys spoke German and they worked out what they were doing, and they gathered, when the Germans went back to their own lines, that they hadn't finished, so these guys went over and had a look, and they said, no, they'll be back again. Bill planned the whole exercise. He took 25, I think, he took his men out quietly and they took up a position. He said being Germans, they'd come along the same track, and he noted how far apart they were, because they do that in case they're . . . and then 'bing,' ten of them are gone. So he worked all of this out, it's all detailed in his award, and they had to stay, and stay and stay and not move as this German patrol came towards them until they were from here to . . . [pointing] there, and then Bill gave the signal by jumping on his feet and throwing a hand grenade, and as soon as he threw the hand grenade – each guy by then was opposite a German. And they were trying to do it quietly; I think there were 40 of them. They killed 24 and took six prisoners

back to their own lines, and one bloke came to, they were carrying him and he started to moan, and that could have given them away, so Bill knocked him on the head. Quizzed about this when they got back and doctors were fixing him up:

'What did you do to him Bill?

'Oh, I just gave him a tap on the head.'

Well, his name was 'Tapper Angus' after that – Bill 'Tapper' Angus.

The couple found that they had a number of friends and acquaintances in common including Malcolm McColm, who had equipped Geoff with the 'magic letter' which enabled him to travel around the world. Malcolm had married one of Alison's closest friends.

Most of Alison's mother's extended family, the Terrys, lived in rural Queensland on large pastoral holdings. Alison had been brought up in a Catholic family of five children, four daughters and a son. Alison's memories of growing up in the Great Depression contrast with Geoff's on the opposite side of the Australian Continent. With her securely employed bank manager father, she doesn't remember really going without anything of significance but she does remember some of the needier children at school. 'It's families like yours . . .' one little girl stated, 'who'll . . .' On one occasion when Alison took a little friend home at lunchtime, Mrs Keogh asked as they were leaving to return to school:

'Do you girls want a fritter?'

'No thanks Mum,' Alison replied, to the dismay of her friend. On reaching school the little girl could not wait to relate her tale.

'You know what she said?' to her expectant companions.

'What?'

'Did we want a frippence!! And SHE said "NO"!'

After Geoff and Alison had been acquainted for a couple of months, Geoff decided, as he had done so many years before, that this was the woman for him 'she really filled a void'. His recollection is that 'it was a mutual thing, it wasn't on bended knee, that sort of stuff, we were getting very fond of each other. In other words, falling in love'. Still not a man to hesitate on matters of the heart.

Alison's recollection is that he proposed on 9 March 1985. Unbeknownst to Geoff, that was the very date on which, all those years before, Bill Angus had proposed to her. Conscious of this poignant irony, Alison says that she replied that she would like to think it over for a day or two. Whether Geoff returned to repeat his proposition the following day or a couple of days later is unclear, but other than in that detail, the rest is history.

An engagement party was held at Alison's daughter, Suzanne's home in Brisbane. Geoff's family in Western Australia were alerted and prepared to celebrate at the home of Geoff's mother, the family headquarters – 15 Joseph Street, West Leederville. During the evening the phone rang, from the West Coast party. It was Geoff's sister, Audrey, to speak to Alison: 'We're drinking a toast! Everyone's here, at Mum's house!' 'The first time we'd spoken,' Alison explains, 'then in the background: "Give it to me!" – it was his mother, Dot.'

'Hello, Mrs Cornish,' Alison began politely.

'So you're going to marry my son?'

'Yes, I'm . . .'

'You'd better look after him; he's a pretty good man you've got hold of! If you don't look after him you'll have me to reckon with!'

'Er, I think he's quite capable of looking after himself.'

'I'll pretend I didn't hear that! Lovely party, everyone enjoying themselves, put you onto Meryl.'

Plans for the wedding progressed, the date having been settled for 18 May 1985, just in time to combine a honeymoon in America with a convention of Rotary International, one of his interests since first joining at Drouin in 1953.

Alison describes the planning as 'not allowing much time to linger over the port'. In organising the coming nuptials, Alison found her fiancé was really not interested in who was to attend. 'They won't come!' he said of his family, seeming oblivious to the possibility that they might nevertheless, be pleased to be invited. 'I don't have any family here,' he protested, 'they're all too far away. I just want you to be there!' Although Alison was disappointed at the lack of Cornish family representatives to be present, she was anxious to please him and there was little more she could do. All five of the couple's children were there.

The occasion was rendered even more colourful by the presence of all the 'Cornish Walkers', Geoff's and Alison's friends from the morning walking programme. The 'Walkers' appeared in force, wearing their 'Heart over Heels' shirts and running shoes, and filled the church with cheering and confetti. A reception was held at the Surfers Paradise Chevron Hotel, the social institution of the district. Alison remembers that the two edifices which marked their union disappeared in the couple of years following their marriage. The Catholic Church and the Chevron Hotel were both demolished to make way for new developments. Not so, thankfully, their marriage.

The couple stayed that night at the Chevron and left on the Sunday morning for Hawaii, where they met up with Geoff's old friend Brewster Morgan. Brewster had arranged accommodation for the newlyweds – the honeymoon suite at the Royal Hawaiian Hotel, the very location of Geoff's altercation with the Canadian officer, so many years ago.

The Royal Hawaiian Hotel, known as the 'Pink Lady' and the 'Pink Palace of the Pacific' is a huge, pink, turreted stucco edifice on Waikiki oceanfront. The hotel's signature theme is pink, still today crystallised in the towels and bed linen. The couple were allocated the Honeymoon Suite. Geoff says: 'Everything was pink. The food was pink. The phone was pink. Anything that wasn't pink was blue. And it was during Alison's "pink phase" too!' Brewster and his companion Cathy took them around the islands so they could see both the natural beauty and the memorabilia of the war. They had a wonderful holiday, surfing, walking, enjoying the sun and the scenery.

After leaving Hawaii, the couple spent a night in San Francisco and had dinner with Geoff's old friend George E Rudolph, who had set up Safeway in Frankston all those years before. During the meal the city experienced an earthquake. 'Their attitude was "it saves you shaking the salt, it does it itself". The locals were nonchalant about minor trembles,' Geoff relates. They travelled on to Salt Lake City, the location of the conference.

As chair of the Rotary 'fellowship for running and fitness' it was Geoff's role to arrange a demonstration of his Walking Programme and the Annual General Meeting of the Fellowship. Geoff recalls:

> Alison gave me a hand. They'd told me that the area was flat, but it turned out to be flat on an angle! We couldn't see our

marker pins over the grass, and the surface was full of gopher holes, worse than rabbit holes.

There was very little attention paid to it. Only five or six turned up for the AGM of the fellowship. That's when I realised that running is not for Rotarians! I dropped that fellowship. I hear that they've now got one for repaired hearts, people who've had bypass or open heart surgery. Perhaps I should . . .

His eyes glaze over. I worry.

21

'Heart over heels'

The couple returned to Surfers Paradise and Geoff moved from his apartment in Whelan Street to Alison's home on the canal off the Little Tallebudgera Creek. He resettled into the medical practice and Alison soon participated in the practice as well as the Walking Programme. They also had many happy weeks with grandchildren. Alison says:

> Geoff taught the children to cast a fishing line and you just couldn't tear them away from the water. One day Alex caught four fish and brought them inside: 'Can we have these for lunch Alla?' They were particularly small fish, just over the limit. Quite ridiculous really. However, Geoff cleaned them and broke them up. We mixed them up with potatoes and made them into fish cakes. The four year old then asked all present: 'How are you enjoying my fish? They just BLEW UP into fish patties! Isn't Alla a good cook?'
>
> He had such patience with the children, never got cross with them or tired of teaching them.

As Alison applied her organisational skills to the day-to-day administration of the quite complex small business, she found a large patient register but a recordkeeping system consisting of a vast number of cardboard boxes. She sorted, filed and gained satisfaction from finally establishing order. Geoff continued his rehabilitation programme alongside his resident 'business manager' and the practice continued to grow. Geoff says that their life together 'just slipped effortlessly into place'. The Daily Walking Programme also expanded. Alison took a major role in the early morning walking sessions at the local oval. Geoff estimates that over 20,000 patients have participated in the rehabilitation programme over two decades.

Geoff's inclination to be an inventor, blossomed. Geoff was, and remains, the master of the 'bright idea'. Be it gym equipment, electronic machinery to monitor heart function, devising an improved bait holder for the crab pot, or a smarter slingshot to deter your backyard crows, Geoff's your man! Alison elaborates: 'A very good brain. Don't know where he got it from. Crazy about astronomy. Just sees something on television and . . .' we can only imagine what on earth he may think of next.

In 1986, a visitor passing the oval on which the walking programme was operating at the time, popped in to have a chat. He was a member of the 'Zipper Club' – the Australian Cardiac Association's interest group of early patients of bypass surgery – who were planning to establish a Gold Coast Branch. The visitor, an Irish born journalist, said that the programme was 'just what was needed' in Canberra. Geoff relates:

> A big talker, really raved about the value of preventive medicine, a launch at Parliament House, a national research foundation . . .'
>
> Alison and I went to Canberra, put a locum into the practice here, and took professional rooms there. We lived there for four months but the formerly thriving Gold Coast Practice began to become a liability. We were writing cheques to support the practice. Alison came back to the Coast and

> I stayed in Canberra. The Canberra rooms cost $350 per week and we had to pay a receptionist as well.
>
> I flew down on Wednesday, on the 6.00 am flight, arriving at eight. Alison ran the morning programme here. I flew back on the last plane from Canberra on Friday night, worked here on Saturday, Monday and Tuesday then back to Canberra for three days. I paid my own air fare and expenses. I knew that what we were doing was good, and thought that eventually they'd pick it up but . . .'
>
> I learnt the bitter political lesson that it doesn't matter what, if it won't get the politicians reelected, they don't follow through. They really weren't ready for preventative medicine.

While Geoff was in Canberra, someone from his past walked into his consulting rooms. It was Eric Stephenson, his mate from the forced march, a member of 'The Firm'. Eric was working in Canberra for the Department of Veterans' Affairs. 'He came storming in and took me straight to lunch at the United Services' Club. I then learned his story. We picked up after forty four years as if it had been a week.'

One of Eric's colleagues had asked did he know of a Dr Geoff Cornish, who'd been in Stalag Luft III, which alerted Eric to Geoff's presence in Canberra.

After the war Eric had completed his medical training, worked in Britain for a time and moved to Australia in 1955. He worked for the RAAF at Sale Air Base in Victoria, Richmond in New South Wales, then in Malaysia and the United States. He returned to Australia and took up a position in Canberra in 1971.

In 2002, Eric celebrated his 80th birthday. The person organising his surprise party at Fairbairn Air force Base, invited Geoff to speak at the function. He accepted. There were letters from all over the place from people who couldn't come – the plaudits were tremendous.

Eric introduced Geoff as 'the person present to have known me longest'. 'What about me?' retorted Eric's wife, Freda.

Geoff recalls his speech:

> I said to myself 'I'll balance this out'. Eric could be a bit of a larrikin, in the POW camp, with the senior nurses. In camp he was called 'Timber'. When he was shot down he landed on the spire of a church – it was a Thursday and he was due to be married on the Saturday. There were lots of jokes about the lengths to which 'Steve' would go, to avoid being married.

To which Eric responds: 'A typical Cornish remark – which I shall treat with complete disdain!'

Eric himself says that he suspects Freda has never forgiven his carelessness, in turning up 'at the wrong church, in the wrong country, on the wrong day!'

It was a thoroughly enjoyable day, a wonderful party. Alison and Geoff drove from the Gold Coast to Canberra for the party, stayed only for the party and commenced their drive back to Queensland before dawn next day. 'Can't just cancel your patients,' Geoff explains.

When Australia was embroiled in the politically potent 'Tampa crisis' – also known as the 'children overboard affair' – the two chatted and seriously considered going public on how things were handled when they were prisoners of war:

> We were able to educate ourselves; we had many opportunities even within our restrictions. We know it from both sides, professionally now as well as from our own experience.
>
> Today's refugees, the 'boat people' are fleeing a regime. If there'd been more people fleeing Germany like this, the war

> would have been over much more quickly. They were the ones with convictions that they couldn't live in the country. We should be showing these young people that they could go back and . . . make the most of their lives. We should educate them, help them to learn skills. We could study anything we wanted; we chose what we would study. These kids could go back to be leaders in their own countries later. Everyone should be able to be in their own country. What a good name that would give Australia.

We shall not know whether the irony would have made an impression upon the Australian public had these men made such a statement. As their own medical education was so substantially enhanced by their experiences as prisoners of war, it would have been fitting that they advise Australia to show a similar generosity of spirit.

22

Maturity

Geoff has continued to nurture his inventiveness. His colleague and old friend, Bruce Satchwell, has been involved with Geoff's inventions for over a decade, first with the firm Micromedical and later with his own company, *Alive Technology*.

Bruce tells us about his work with Dr Cornish:

> Geoff had no way of collecting the data from patients' electrocardiograms (ECGs) so that he could validate that what he thought was happening, was in fact happening. We developed a product based on his idea, called *HeartTel*, using a little box which the patient wears for a day. It differs from regular heart monitors in that we had software which allows you to measure the exact heart rate, beat for beat. It is crucial to Geoff's system that the load is very strictly controlled so you need to check that the heart rate is staying constant. We wrote software which enabled the ECG information, stored in the device, to be downloaded into a programme called *CardioView* that analyses it and prints out a report. That took about a year.
>
> Another design, a product that the patient could buy and keep, was *CARD*. Like *HeartTel* but more long term; if you've a heart problem you have it at home, monitor yourself and your exercise and send the data to the doctor. Geoff was also quite involved in that project.

> We also helped modify the thing that goes 'beep' in the middle of the oval. He had an older one – we made it into one that sounds like a bird. The current one is called *tweety one*.
>
> We are now working on a wireless heart monitor, which uses a GPS, so that at the oval Geoff can monitor people up to 2–300 metres away. We're testing it at the morning programme. Also with a GPS, a patient can do their exercise on their own, measure how fast they're walking on their own. They don't have to do it in a group they can do it anywhere. By using a GPS you can do it without the marks. People don't really know what one unit of exercise means; a brisk walk means different things to everyone, and if you walk slowly you don't get any benefits at all.

In 1996 Geoff became aware of an irritation on the side of his head. After Alison's making several humorous remarks as to the possible causes, it became clear that it might be another melanoma. Testing revealed this to be so and the offending growth was removed by a dermatologist and exhaustively tested. It was another primary growth, not the possible secondary tumour which all were dreading. Late in 1998, whilst attending a meeting of his local branch of the Australian Medical Association (AMA), Geoff experienced a shooting pain at the back of his head, above his left ear. He quickly sought tests and again found evidence of cancer. Further examination revealed a clutch of small malignant growths, necessitating radical surgery followed by radiotherapy. Following that treatment at Brisbane's Mater Hospital he was symptom free until 2004.

Geoff's medical practice continues at the present time and he remains disinclined to retire. Alison, his ever patient if sometimes exasperated wife, proudly shows me a greeting card some twelve years old, in which he promises to 'definitely retire this year'.

His activities in the community also continue – Surfers Paradise Rotary, the Surfers Paradise RSL, Gold Coast Committee on the Ageing, the Air Crew Association and Ex Prisoners of War Association and, as a result of his marriage to Alison, he is an honorary 'Rat of Tobruk'.

Anzac Day remains an institution for the Cornishes – in earlier days, the 'Gunfire Breakfast' at Surfers RSL in the company of many prominent citizens and ex-service personnel, including the former Premier of Queensland, Rob Borbidge. These days, many earlier attendees have departed, but in 2004 when the author accompanied our subjects, the crowd of young people was greater than ever before. As usual Geoff was interviewed by media representatives and reported in the State Daily Press.

Geoff continues to follow his professional dreams. Several of his brainchildren are still gestating. In collaboration with Griffith University's Gold Coast Campus, two inventions are in the later stages of testing with the potential to be realised and marketed in the near future.

23

WHAT GOES AROUND

Geoff attended celebrations in London for three anniversaries of The Great Escape. The first was in the company of his first wife Myra, in 1969; the second, in 1994, to which he travelled with Eric Stephenson; the third, in 2004 with Alison.

What has happened to the characters who have peopled this story, whom our subject has known over the years? Many have 'come around again', and many others have achieved fame or interest in other worlds entirely.

When Geoff and Eric travelled to London in 1994 to attend the fiftieth anniversary of the Great Escape, they participated in a celebratory function at the RAF Club in Piccadilly and a memorial service at the Church of St Clement Danes in The Strand. Eric then travelled to Poland to view the memorials at Sagan. He remembers that:

> The Poles had done a lot to resurrect the memorial for the 50 . . . which the Russians had nearly destroyed.
>
> [It was] beautifully reconstructed; a chain link fence protected it.
>
> [Then we went to the] British military cemetery in Posnan. It was very significant. I was quite complimentary to the Polish people – it's a very poor part of the country there, and one of them said to me in response, I've never forgotten:

> 'You must not forget Air Vice Marshall, that you were the only people we knew were still fighting for us!'
>
> They heard us flying over and dropping bombs on those German cities. They could hear us in Sagan when we were bombing Berlin, 100 kilometres away.
>
> He gave me to understand that it made quite a difference to their morale because they had absolutely nothing else to hope for; the Germans never told them anything except that they were winning, and they knew that things were different.

After the London reunion in March 1994, whilst Eric was visiting Poland, Geoff joined his old friend Mike Horsfall, still living in his same beautiful country home near Birmingham, close to the family business, Latch and Batchelor, Cable-makers. Mike and Geoff went to visit Pop Coventry. Pop was now in failing health, being so much older than they. Geoff travelled by train to the outer suburbs of London to see 'Conk' Canton.

He had promised to call at Berlin on his way back to Australia to visit Frau Gottschalk, mother of his friend, Nick. Whilst in London, Geoff was charged with keeping their former Senior British Officer from Stalag Luft III North, 'Wings' Day, sober for the official functions. Day was to lead the march. Having been a 'lad' and a half since his youth and always a formidable drinker, Day presented quite a challenge. 'They told me it was my medical duty,' Geoff recants, 'so I had to do my best'. Geoff remembers Wings Day as having had the good fortune to thrice marry wealthy, elegant women. At some point Day mentioned that he had met and maintained contact with Hermann Glemnitz after the war. Geoff was enthralled. 'I'll write to him,' Day promised, 'and tell him you're here and going to Germany,' but appeared to never give his words another thought. Eric relates that they learned that Glemnitz had made his way to the British zone of Berlin and was recognised by a former RAF officer who helped him to find a job as a security guard or 'Sicherheit Agent' in Britain after the war. The same legend had it that Glemnitz had retired on a British pension!

When Geoff's aircraft reached Berlin, Frau Gottschalk was waiting, easily recognisable by the red flower in her coat lapel. Standing beside her was Glemnitz! 'Crikey' Geoff exclaimed. 'Wings Day told me to come,' Glemnitz declared. 'We go on pub crawl!'

Geoff explained that he was staying with Frau Gottschalk and leaving at dawn next morning. His hostess insisted that she would be retiring early. 'No problem', responded Glemnitz, 'I'll come and fetch you later.' So Geoff and Frau Gottschalk had a wonderful meal and discussed the past and her son's success in Australia. The Frau produced a gift which she asked Geoff to take to her son – a tiny gold nugget inherited from his grandfather who had mined in the United States during the gold rush there. Geoff pressed it into his tin of Australian, black 'Nugget' shoe polish and presented it to her son Nick in that very packaging.

Shortly after nine, Geoff's escort arrived for an evening in Berlin's nightspots and the pair left to catch up on one another's lives since they were last together – which was when the Americans were transferred out of North into the new South Compound, prior to the Great Escape. Glemnitz had gone with the Americans.

In 1965 Hermann Glemnitz was guest at a reunion of the USAAF in Dayton, Ohio. His appreciation of the invitation and a succinct account of his fate after the war are presented in his letter to American friends, now posted on the World Wide Web. Extracts from the beautifully handwritten, reproduced image, are reproduced below.

You have made me very happy with your very nice letter and copy of the Chicago tribune which I received shortly before Xmas although I think that there are too many lorrels [sic] for me, I only did what any other disciplined soldier would or should have done . . . I am very proud to call you and so many more of the ex-kriegies my friends. 1965 . . . was one of the cheerfullest and most happiest years of my life because of the reunion in Dayton where I met so many old kriegies who convinced me that everyone of them had not forgotten and liked me.

Before Moosburg was handed over to the American forces I took my some 60 soldiers under my command and marched south as I didn't wanted to become a prisoner without fighting. In May I had to surrender, became a prisoner myself, and was released end of June 1945. My home town was Breslau, Silesia . . . and I made my way afoot appr 650 kilometres. I made 30 km per day . . . I was well trained by you kriegies and marched most of the time at night and through the woods. When I reached the border of Silesia the Poles stopped me and would not let me pass. Waiting two days in rain I took the chance and jumped onto a passing and slow moving Russian goods train and so reached the other side. It was end of July 45 when, although very tired and with lice I arrived in Breslau where I found my family in good health. They thought that I was dead . . . Life amongst the Poles was unbearable for me . . . as soon as I was on the street I was attacked by them.

I was a wealthy man in pre-war times and possessed a block of 17 flats. And not a penny of debt. I could live easily on the rent of the house but I saw I could not stay in Breslau. I packed a rucksack and left my home country as a refugee. After a time in the Russian zone where they wanted to make me a farmer I landed in Berlin where I started right from the scratch and I must say that I was successful.

Cordial greetings, sincerely, Hermann and Hilde.

24

Due recognition

In the fiftieth anniversary year of Geoff Cornish's graduation as a doctor, Griffith University, Queensland awarded him its highest tribute to a citizen, Doctor of the University.

The Cornish Walking Program was originally devised by Dr Cornish for his wife following her second heart operation in 1972. It is a community based program which encourages people to exercise as part of their heart rehabilitation program, and can be duplicated anywhere in the world. The program received international recognition at the Fourth World Congress on Cardiac Rehabilitation in 1998.
Dr Cornish continues to devote his time, energy and resources to the community. At 80 year of age, he works over 12 hours a day conducting the Cornish Walking Program, 'Hearts Over Heels'. He has an active medical practice in Benowa, focussing primarily on older Australians.
In 1993 he was named 'Gold Coast Citizen of the Year' for his contributions to the Gold Coast community. In the same year he was awarded a Medal of the Order of Australia (OAM) for 'his contribution to Medicine, particularly in the field of Heart Rehabilitation'.
In recognition of his outstanding service to the Gold Coast region, the Gold Coast City Council named a two kilometre walk along Broadbeach in his honour.

Professor Greg Gass made available the introductory citation, shown above. The award was presented on 5 October 2002, by Chancellor Leneen Forde. Geoff's speech to the graduates is presented below.

> The ambience of excitement, optimism and happiness is almost palpable. The air vibrates with impatience to get on with the exciting part of your lives now that one of the biggest hurdles of all has been successfully conquered. In keeping with the furious pace of most aspects of today's happenings it will be tempting to begin in top gear and proceed straight into overdrive. Please, please, pause to catch your breath, get your bearings, and quietly review your life and the philosophy that is now yours. Then chart what you believe to be the best course for your future.
>
> Not all knowledge can be found on the World Wide Web. You will learn from every experience you ever have. Graduation is your passport to a lifetime of learning.
>
> I have been reminded of how the world is constantly changing, by my recent reading. Galaxies still evolving have been identified beyond what were thought of as the outer limits of the universe. Machines have been made which are working while attached to living human red blood cells. Within these examples lie a wealth of new careers. Continuing to learn in your career pathway should always provide that tingling feeling in the pit of your stomach.
>
> Subtle changes in direction are usually of your own choosing and carefully planned. The most drastic are forced upon you by persons or events over which you have no control.
>
> In my own case the declaration of war on Germany sent everything spinning and plans were in limbo. After training for one year, I was posted to bomber squadron, as a pilot. Six months later, I lost a deadly struggle with Messerschmitt night fighters over Holland. All my crew were killed, and I became a prisoner of war. Over the next few years in 'The Great Escape' camp, I had the opportunity to learn the basic essentials of medicine from one of our own Prisoner of War doctors. This put my life back on track.

> Now, having been in medical practice for 50 years I still have that tingling in the pit of my stomach. As Fred Hollows said: 'Try and leave the world a better place.'
>
> Geoff Cornish MBBS OAM 5 October 2001

The awarding of the honour coincided with the fiftieth anniversary of his graduation and was to prompt the author's request to document Geoff's life. Not only was her request granted but she assisted Geoff to finalise his speech. She recalls:

> It was the first time I visited his home; it was to work on his speech for the Griffith graduation. He talked and I taped and took notes. He mused as to what one ought to say to graduating students. We almost covered his whole life just in that exercise.
>
> Over two weeks we drafted and redrafted. On the afternoon of the ceremony I was printing out the final copy for Geoff to use on the stage and as I stood up to leave home, he phoned with more changes. I was late and the manager took my notes to Geoff on the podium. I felt so privileged to be participating, I felt the thrills myself.

The occasion marked the beginning of an extraordinary journey which has culminated in the publication of this book.

March 2004 marked the sixtieth anniversary of the Great Escape. Shortly before the anniversary and in anticipation of worldwide recognition of the event, the television company

Nine Australia approached Geoff and his wife Alison with a proposal that they accompany Tara Brown (presenter), Stephen Taylor (producer) and the current affairs team to London and Poland. They would together produce a documentary for Nine's *Sixty Minutes* current affairs programme, to commemorate the Great Escape. Needless to say the proposal was accepted with pleasure and the couple departed with the television team. A memorable fortnight followed.

On arriving in London, the couple were installed at a Leicester Square Hotel where they would stay for the duration. They attended all of the anniversary events in London, of which parts were filmed for the television programme. Celebrations at the Imperial War Museum in London saw Geoff as a key guest and speaker. The RAF Club at Piccadilly again hosted the official RAF reunion of the last surviving POWs.

Arrangements had been made for Geoff to visit the Netherlands and be reacquainted with Wilhelmina Beckers Mertens, eldest daughter of the family into whose home Geoff was welcomed after his crash. Wilhelmina, now aged 80, lives in Maastricht with her husband. Her brother Martin lives nearby but these days has a condition which impairs his speech. He was nonetheless most excited to meet Geoff again. The television crew organised for the group to meet at Wilhelmina's house where Geoff would surprise her by knocking at the door, carrying a large bunch of flowers. The group were then to proceed to the area where the family had lived and Geoff had parachuted to ground, in the town of Nunhem. All went according to plan.

The reunion was an emotional one. Wilhelmina was strongly of the view that it should have taken place years before. She had written to Geoff's home in Perth after the war, but he had left for Melbourne and she had received no response. Although Geoff had spoken of his friends many times over the years it was only after the near completion of research for this book that the contact was re-established.

When the group arrived at the spot where Geoff had landed, little resembled that evening sixty three years ago. There was no chicken pen and no house, but the canal was still there and the area was green and tree-covered. Wilhelmina was able to add to the story of that April night.

The experience confirmed Geoff's' view that learning of his collision during this research had arranged the jigsaw of his life into a coherent picture. The new information stitched together a long–incomplete tapestry.

Wilhelmina showed Geoff the statue that the villagers had created in memory of the soldiers who had died there. The Dutch made one statue for all – 'they were all fighting for a cause'. The tall construct has a stone for each soldier, every name is engraved and flying birds symbolically circle the apex.

After the war, Wilhelmina tells the visitors, she and 300 or so children were sent to Scotland to recover from starvation. At that time the northern part of France was still under occupation. Britain was still in blackout, as her homeland had been for so long.

The trip to Poland was something else altogether. Geoff had not revisited Sagan, any of the prison locations, nor any of the places which directly reflected the memories of his mates, despite how large those memories had loomed for sixty years. The site of Stalag Luft III and North Compound in particular was eerie, spiritual, saddening and yet in a sense exhilarating.

The television documentary portraying these events was sensitively produced and emotionally moving. Geoff was escorted and interviewed by journalist Tara Brown as he made his way through the various locations and experiences.

The group visited the site of Stalag Luft III, finding only

ruins. There were visible remains only of the theatre, the water reservoir and one tunnel entrance – that of *Dick*, the third of the *Tom Dick and Harry* trio. That entrance was unearthed only in September 2003 when the makers of a documentary about Stalag Luft III dug a 10 metre pit at the exact place where it had been. Deep inside the entrance to Dick archaeologists found some old Klim tins forged into piping, the concrete slab which had covered the entrance, and one of the forger's rubber stamps carved from the heel of an airman's boot.

Examining a plan of the former camp while standing on the site, the visitors marvelled at the distance that the *Harry* tunnel had covered – now marked by a pebble path; the tragedy of the tunnel being ten metres short; and the fact that the escapers had managed to traverse the gap outside the tunnel whilst under the full surveillance of the guards.

Geoff showed them where the individual compounds had stood, reiterated the length of time that the men had spent in each, and laughed with the film crew about his attempt to escape as the Russian with the treetop. 'One day after that I was in the cooler!' Tara commented on his audacity. Geoff retorted: 'If you saw an opportunity, you took it!'

The surrounding countryside appeared much the same as it had in photographs of the stalag days, peppered with conifers and light undergrowth, and was very, very cold. Bill Fordyce, another Australian accompanying the *Sixty Minutes* team, recalled his near panic at being about to climb off the trolley to exit as escaper number 86, when the tunnel was discovered. He had to reverse backwards the length of the tunnel – as quickly as possible, which was very slowly – and leave some of his personal treasures behind.

After visiting Sagan the group travelled to the British Military Cemetery at Posnan, where all of the murdered escapers are commemorated. On entering the cemetery, the first memorial Geoff saw was that of Charles Hall, his escape replacement: 'The first one I saw, Steve,' he lamented to the television producer. He was visibly distressed and tearful and again repeated the story of the exchange, and his own emotions after the tragedy.

He saw the memorials of so many more of his mates, and told anecdotes of Roger Bushell, Al Hake, Danny Krol – 'boy, could he dig!' – Jimmy Catanach and Tim Walenn.

Geoff returned to Australia with a small package of sand from *Dick*. After quarantine the sand was returned to him, to be shared between the Australian War Memorial and his own collection of memorabilia.

In Poland, plans are afoot to build a memorial which will include a structure at each end of the tunnel *Harry*. The entrance structure will show visitors a 'below ground view of what the prisoners experienced' and a sky view symbolising hope and freedom. The second structure, at the exit, will demonstrate the 10 metre shaft which the prisoners would ascend in order to leave. Each structure will be visible from the other and the space between will indicate the underground distance which the men had to traverse. This project is the goal of the Great Escape Memorial Project Committee, an international group which has received funding from around the world. The plans were unveiled by Carrie Tobolski, the granddaughter of one of the murdered escapers, at Zagan on 24 March 2004, during the City's VIP Reception for the sixtieth Anniversary.

EPILOGUE

On Friday 5 March 2004, Geoffrey phoned me before dawn.

'Come for breakfast, I've something to tell you!'

'What is it?'

'You'll find out when you get here.'

I hope desperately that the on-again, off-again trip is now a goer. I arrive and the kitchen is all action. Eggs, bread, cheeses. The dog scurrying under our feet; Alison fussing. Geoff with ingredients, frypans, dishes, and plates. 'Sit down.' I comply and move to the seat under the window.

'I've had a CAT scan. I've got secondaries.'

'Where?'

'Lungs and rib cage.'

'What will they do?'

'Nothing.'

I fail to grasp the significance of this, assuming the growths must be below critical size. We look at each other and Alison starts waving to me from the kitchen. I don't understand. She makes sure Geoff can't see her gesturing.

He looks serious and is quieter than is his normal wont. I go quiet too.

'So, what will happen?' I ask.

'Don't know,' he says.

♡

The past week has been chaotic and disappointing without any of this. The invitation to attend the *Great Escape* London celebrations has not been backed by an offer of travel and accommodation; so attending is really beyond the couple's means. Amongst all this, the medical tests have been carried out. Geoff and Alison attended the oncologist yesterday and Alison tells me that he has declared there is no hope.

Phone calls come and go. It seems there is a possibility that a trip may be arranged by the television programme *Sixty Minutes*. When this begins to look more like go than stop, I insist on taking Alison and the puppy to have its shots. On Saturday morning we drive in the blinding rain, have the injections and return home. The trip appears to be on, but we're still not absolutely sure. We talk at length about arrangements – obtaining passports quickly, what to do with the puppy, who will keep an eye on the house. We have a sumptuous breakfast again, cooked by us all with Geoff at the helm.

I leave to drive home, with all this slowly sinking in. Yesterday I was strong; there were things I could do; I knew that I was contributing. Today I just feel sad and teary. I drive down the highway, towards home, and as I often do, remember things according to landmarks. The *D'Arcy Arms* where we had such a lovely Christmas meal; the turnoff to the oval where the walkers meet at Broadbeach; the bank at Miami where I stopped for money, and had to wait until the end of the interview tape that I was replaying as I drove home, the story of Geoffrey meeting Myra – the dance – 'I'm puffed'; the place at Burleigh where their car broke down; and my dog park near home where puppy *Heart* likes to run with the big dogs.

By now tears are streaming down my cheeks. I am heading home alone and I must face up to what is happening to my friends.

How long will it take? Surely it's not true that nothing can be done. What will happen to Alison? Although she's been so strong, she lives for Geoff. She wants to protect him and he can't bear to be mollycoddled. Alison is becoming more distracted.

The trip comes through. They have a wonderful time, love and are loved by the television team and come home happy, exhausted and ill. Geoffrey has near pneumonia, Alison is tired, bewildered and incubating a chest condition. It is wonderful to have them back. Over the coming weeks Geoff investigates further the possibility of cancer treatments. The local specialists are unwavering in their views, already expressed, that there is no hope. Geoff's research turns up the possibility of an experimental, new vaccine treatment, available only through a University at Newcastle, near Sydney. The pair fly down for a day and return with a freeze pack of vaccine.

He will have the vaccine treatment from his own GP fortnightly, and after a time, intersperse it with chemotherapy. After a week recovering from pneumonia he returns to work, insistent that he must retrieve the backlog in his patient caseload. He seems uncharacteristically unaware that his wife is also ill.

By July the vaccine-only treatment period is complete and the chemotherapy begins. Geoff still insists on working at his practice although Alison attends the morning walking programme at the oval. I cannot believe that this is really happening. Geoff starts to be hit by the chemotherapy. He's fine for a few days after the first two-hour dose but by the following week he is exhausted. I search the internet and learn that this is the pattern.

I sit in the usual corner of the living room with Geoff. He is on my left, I on his right, so he can hear me through his good ear. We have sat thus for hundreds of hours over the past two years. All our confidences are here, shared with my pen, tape recorder and sometimes the dogs. What a journey it's been into the corners of the couple's lives. I have felt the fighters strafing overhead, swallowed the last bits of eggshell. I remember the anatomy school; the streets of Croydon, Hawthorn and South Yarra.

Geoffrey has generously shared every detail of the places to which he has been prepared to let me go. He has always been the gatekeeper. Alison has also shared information unstintingly, unselfconsciously in the way that some women do. The responsibilities and obligations of the biographer are real indeed. There have been times that Alison has said to me: 'You and Geoff are so alike'. I still do not know what she means.

We have here a man who has directed all of his life to his passion – medicine. Medicine became the driver when he was a very young boy and intensified to fever pitch in adolescence. One dream after another promised to make it come true. What a detour it took to arrive there. To spend four years of a war locked away unable to fight the bastards, to be confined to playing games with the human detritus of the enemy while your mates led adventures such as the *Dam Busters*.

Geoffrey Cornish's life is a real story of G and D, from the '*has guts +*' of the RAF recruiting assessment to his determination to find ways of turning every day into a learning experience, in the most unlikely of circumstances.

'How does it all look now? How would you want to be remembered? Hypothetically, fifty years on, there's no heart disease any more. It's all been quashed by lifestyle, genetic engineering and the brilliant new

technology of growing new organs from stem cells. What do you wish to be remembered for?' I ask.

'That I'd made an original and important contribution to medicine. That's all.'

'Nothing else, only medicine?' I probe.

'No, that's enough. A very exalted achievement, profession. I don't look for recognition . . . or payback or anything. No. Nothing else.'

'If it was Sue and I talking about her dad? Family; all the people whose lives you've touched, like Ivor Hanger and Noel did for you?' I try further.

'I think it goes back to my little motto you know about expanding your life always along the four different avenues and if you can present what you've done, how you've done it so that people say "that is the way to go" then . . . then alright, I've incorporated Christianity into it as well.'

'And the most pleasure? Four things you've loved most?'

'I couldn't ask for another happy marriage, could I? I've had two beauties! And as a result of that, a lovely family and a place in society where you enjoyed it and they enjoyed having you. That's about it, I think.'

Biography is sometimes described as telling the stories of ordinary people in extraordinary situations; of making the ordinary, extraordinary. I see it as conveying the elements of a life, to be interpreted as it refracts within the eye of the reader.

I watch my friends now, and what friends they have become, as has the little border collie. We are all older. Wiser, frailer, more grateful.

These two extraordinary octogenarians are a story just in the here and now, even without the past: pottering; creating;

looking after others and each other; denying their own frailty in the enduring hope of 'going on forever'.

There were two occasions on which Geoff went quiet: when my research uncovered that his plane had exploded after the crash and the day he was told his cancer was untreatable.

They are both becoming forgetful, like my parents did. We have our share of muddles, mistaken appointment times, misplaced photos, articles and keys. The more things change the more they stay the same, as the French say. Forgetfulness is common.

I sometimes go home gloomy now. A wonderful experience is coming to an end. We are all three changing; the book is complete. It will be launched and we will all be launched into another phase.

I have written this story in a manner which I hope will enable the reader to create their own picture of Geoffrey and his fellows. It is intended that the space between the lines generate as much meaning as the words themselves. In an effort to 'show not tell' and to elicit the active participation of the reader I have used the personalities' own words and voices wherever possible. Where ambiguity of outcome or intent was evident to me I have preserved it without corruption, for the reader to focus their own kaleidoscope within the world that we have visited together.

INDEX

Ackroyd, Dr John 174
AD 789 58, 61
Adolph 69
Air Crew Association 209
Albany 2
Alcantara 136
Alderminster 41
Alive Technology 207
Alsatian dogs 71, 72, 73, 90
Angus, Alison 192
Angus, Bill 'Tapper' 197
Ansty 39
Anzac Day 22, 209
Appell 92, 99, 100
Australia House 37, 38, 136
Australian High Commissioner 37
Australian Medical Association 208
Australian War Memorial 220
Avro Anson 47, 49
Aylesbury 40

B–51 120
B–52 Super Fortresses 115
Bader, Douglas 74, 75, 76
Ballarat 1
Barrett, Bill 76
Barth 67, 68, 70, 71, 74, 85, 94
Battle of Britain 47, 52
Bayliss, NS 29, 32, 144
BBC 92
Bearham, Dr George 166
Beaufort 102
Beilngries 124
Belaria 102, 104–5, 109–10
Benelong 187
Benez, ex-President 48
Bernhard, Prince 48
Big X 72, 79, 91
Blackboy Hill 2
Blackmore, 'Dot' *see* Cornish, Dot
boat people 205
Bomber Command 46
Borbidge, Rob 209
Bordeaux 55
Bow Street 45
Boyle's 179
brains trust 97
Brickhill, Paul 87, 97
Brisbane River 1
Bristol Blenheim 50
British Military Cemetery, Posnan 219
Bronte Park, Tasmania 167
Brown, Tara 218
Bryant 40–1, 152
Bryant and May 40
Buchanan, Mr Russell 160

Buckley, Jimmy 63, 65, 66
Bushell, Roger 63, 65, 66, 72, 78, 83, 91, 103, 220

Cambridge 38–9, 66
Canton, Conk 122
CARD 207
CardioView 207
Carroll, Tim 87, 107
Casey, Mike 65, 66
CAT 221
Catanach, Jimmy 220
Chamberlain, PM Neville 35
Chandler, Tommy 21
Charmy Down 57
Cherub 70, 75
CIG 179
City of Benares 35
Colditz Castle 75
Colombo 35, 145
Commodore Perry 1
Commonwealth 6
Commonwealth Games 1962 180
Coolgardie safe 20
Cornish, Alison 192–200, 202–5, 208–10, 217, 221–4
Cornish, Audrey *see* Johnson
Cornish, Dot 3–15, 18, 19, 30, 102, 144, 155–6, 192, 198
Cornish, Fred 2–13, 29, 30, 34, 98, 144, 155
Cornish, Gordon 7, 8, 12, 19, 20, 34, 64, 144, 155
Cornish, Gwenith *see* Williams, Gwenith
Cornish, Joe 3, 5, 7, 34
Cornish, John 1
Cornish, Keith 7, 10, 13, 18, 20, 73, 102, 144
Cornish, Louisa 1
Cornish, Myra 150–163, 165–7, 170–1, 173, 176–8, 180–91, 210
Cornish, Roy 7, 12, 19, 180
Cornish, Susan 1
Cornish, William 1, 2, 4, 14, 18, 144
Coventry 39, 116, 147, 149, 152
Coventry, Pop 104, 109, 120, 122, 126, 211
Cranwell 43, 44, 46, 65, 74, 146
crayfish story 45
Crossman, John 35
Cuthbert 123, 124, 126, 128
CWA 168

D'Arcy Arms 222
Dachau 130
Daily Mirror 68
Dam Busters 50, 224
Dandenong 180
Danube 124
Day, 'Wings' 65–6, 86–7, 131, 190, 195, 211–12
DC3 Dakotas 133
DDT 134
de Gaulle, General 48
Dean and Dawson 85
Denmark, Crown Prince of 76, 91
DFC *see* Distinguished Flying Cross
Dick 219, 220
Dimwits 69
Distinguished Flying Cross 50, 74
doughnuts 129
Douglas DC–3 132
Dowse, Sydney 82
Drouin 171
Dulag Luft 63, 65, 66, 72, 74, 78, 112
Dummköpfe 86
Dunlap 122

Dunlop, Sir Edward 'Weary' 161, 174
Durand, Arthur 113, 115
Durchgangslager der Luftwaffe *see* Dulag Luft
Düsseldorf 58–9, 61, 111

East Compound 74–6, 83–5
Egypt 2
Eindhoven 58, 63
Empire Air Training Scheme 30
Empire theatre 22
Enschede 111
Escape Committee 91, 103
Eureka Stockade 1
euthanasia 130
Evening Standard 37
Ex Prisoners of War Association 209

Faithful Annie 47
ferrets 68, 69, 71, 93
Ferry, Rod 97
Fighter Command 50
fisch salbe 101
flying suitcase *see* Hampden
flying tadpole *see* Hampden
Forde, Chancellor Leneen 215
Fordyce, Bill 106
Four Square Club 26
Frank, Anna 63
Frankfurt am Main 63, 65
Frankston 180
Freetown 36
'frippence' story 198
Frommel 76
Fruehoff, Orry 1, 70

Galle Face 146
Gammelsdorf 125
Gass, Professor Greg 215
Gaumont 152
Geneva Convention 45, 65, 72–3, 87, 113–14, 119
German Bribery Department 78, 80
Gestapo 62, 94–6, 103, 107, 111, 145
Gibson, Guy DFC 50, 51
Gironde 56
Gitte 76, 147–8
Glemnitz 69, 84–6, 91–3, 128, 211–13
Glenfern Antiques 178
Goebels 76
Goering 111
Gold Coast Committee on the Ageing 209
Goldicote Manor 41, 152
Goodrich, Colonel 109
Goons 68, 119, 122, 123
goony birds 133
Gottschalk, Frau 211
Gottschalk, Nick 169, 172, 212
Gotttschalk, Helen 182
Graf Spee 36
Great Depression 8, 20, 197
Great Escape 72, 77–9, 97, 107, 184, 210–16
  Memorial Project Committee 220
Great Escapers, The 87
Griese 69
Griffith University 209, 214
Guest, Tommy 67, 70, 72
Guy Fawkes 22
Gwen, Auntie, Gwenith, *see* Williams
Gwennap, Cornwall 1
GWR 57

Hake, Al 82, 220
Halifaxes 115
Hall, Charles 85, 103, 106, 220

Hampden 50, 52, 55–61
Handley Page Herefords 50
Hanger, Ivor 25, 144
Harry 105, 219, 220
Hawaii 133, 138–9, 141, 146, 200
Heart 222
Heart over Heels 199
HeartTel 207
Heath Robinson 41
Heinkel 48
Heron, Helen 39
Heron, Jim 39, 40
Hesse, Corporal 82
Hickham Military Airfield 138
Higgins, Jimmy 83, 94
Hildebrandt 100
Hill, Geoff 82
Hill, Joe 70
Hinsich 111
Hitler Youth 131
HMS Royal Oak 37
Holocaust 130
Horsfall, Mike 111, 118, 211
Hudson 41
Hughes, Kent 31, 154
Hume-Cooke, Keith 159, 163
Hundfürher 82

It's all pensionable time 116
Ivan der Schrecklich/the Terrible 91

Jack the Butler 40
James, Jimmy 78
Japanese surrender 140
Jesus College 38–9
Jindivik 186
Johnson, Audrey 7, 9, 14–17, 20, 64, 144–5
Johnson, Brian 10

Kahuku 139
Kalgoorlie 1, 18, 121
Kangaroo Paw 10
Keeley, Martin and Joan 184
Keen Type 69
Kennedy, Graham 178
Kerr, Professor Alex 13, 22
Kings Park 10, 143
Klim 83, 219
Knocker, F/L 39
kriegie 65, 92, 99, 115, 119, 120

Lady Frances Ryder Scheme 40
Lancasters 115, 133
Landshut 132
Larkin, Wing Commander 96
Latch and Batchelor 211
Lawrence Sheriff School 149
lazarett 101, 104, 110
Lindholme 52–3, 55–6
Luftwaffe 52, 59, 65, 100, 102, 106

Macrossan, Justice
Chief Justice of Queensland 38
Macrossan, Pat 36, 38
mangels 125
Mantell, Dr Mike 179
24–25 March 1946 105
March 5, 2004 221
Marcinkus, René 77
Massey SBO 106
McColm Malcolm 136, 197
McIntosh, Jack 40
McKean, Dr Barry 179
McKinley, F/L 49
ME–262 109
melanoma 28, 186, 208
Merlin 115
Mertens, Martin 62, 217
Mertens, Mr (father) 62
Mertens, Wilhelmina Beckers 62, 217, 218

Messerschmitt 59, 61, 66, 77
Mexico 137
Micromedical 207
Military Cross 196
Military Medal 2, 30
mink coat 185
Mombassa 35
Monger's Lake 4, 16, 18, 19
Monteuuis 99–104, 109, 10
Moosburg 119, 128
Moreton Bay 1
Morgan, Brewster 133, 138, 200
Mosquito 112
Muhlhausen 125
Mustang 112

National Heart Foundation 177
Nazi 52, 114, 125, 132
Neer 61
Neumarkt 119
Neustadt 125
New Zealand House 136
Newman, Tim 136
Nine Australia 217
Normandy Landings 108
North Compound 74, 87–8, 92, 102–11, 218
Norwood, Muriel 160
Nunhem 217
Nuremberg 112, 119
Nuremberg–Langwasser' 113

O'Reillys 40
Oahu 139
October 13, 1939 37
Oder River 109
Oflag 67
Old Perth Road 15
Orama 34–36, 154
OTU 50
Oxfords 43

Panzer Division 125
Parker, Bush 82, 95
Parkes, Granny 40
Patterson, Jock 67
Patton, General George 118, 128, 131–2
Peenemunde 94
Pegg, Mr. 39
Pellet, Colonel 113–14
Penguin trousers 93
Perry, Adele 162, 170, 174, 178, 183–4, 190–1
Perth 2
Perth Secondary Boys' Technical School 21
Peterkin, Doug 31
Pieber 69, 85, 89, 92, 106
Pine Ranch 181
Pink Palace of the Pacific 140, 200
plank roads 15
Pöling 119
Pope, Lois 18
Posnan 210
Postern 126
Powell, Dave 58, 61, 63
Prahran Market 162
Prince of Wales 7
Protecting Power 113

Quamby Hotel 1, 59
quisling 103

RAF Club, Piccadilly 210
Ramsay, Sir James 188
Rat of Tobruk 195, 209
Ratcliffe, Jack 57–8, 60
RCAF 138
RCH Orthopaedic Hospital 183
Reach for the Sky 74
Reath and Lapsley 23, 32

Red Cross Blood Bank 168–9
Red Cross parcels 69–78, 80–3, 109–13, 122–7
Reese, Lieutenant H 61
River Cam 38
Robertson, Ann and Graham 160
Roitzaak, Unteroffizier W 61
Roosevelt 126
Rotary International 173, 189, 199, 200
Rotary Surfers Paradise 209
Royal Air Force 30
Royal Hawaiian Hotel 140, 200
Royal Melbourne Hospital 190
Royle, Paul 70
RSL 2, 22, 155, 163, 164, 175, 209
Rubberneck 69, 94, 105
Rudolph, George E 200
Ruhr 50, 63
Russians 72–3, 83, 88–90, 111–14, 132, 164, 210
Ryder *see* Lady Frances Ryder Scheme

Sagan 74, 112, 210, 220
Salt Lake City 200
Sammy 118
San Diego 137
Saschenhausen 106
Savoy House 38
SBO 65
Schäffer 28
Scharnhorst 57
school medals, Fred's 2
Sierra Leone 36
Silesia 74
Sixty Minutes 217, 222
Slatter, Jack 31, 154
slave labour *see* Russians
Smallwood ,'Pud' 21, 50
Smith, Darby 164
Sons of Soldiers League 22
Spitfire XI 111
Squadrons:
50 Squadron 52, 53
57 Squadron 66
92 Squadron 66
106 Squadron 52
601 'Millionaires' Squadron, 66
Eagle Squadron 138
squitters 124
SS 36, 111, 120
SS Ashlea 36
SS Clement 36
SS Newton Beech 36
St Athan 46, 47, 49, 57
St Clement Danes 210
St Eval 56
St Lucia 1
Stalag 67
Stalag Luft I 67, 70, 71, 84, 91
Stalag Luft III 48, 72, 74, 78, 204, 211, 218, 219
Stalag Luft III East 74
Stalag Luft III North 87, 96, 105, 107, 109, 211, 218
Stalag XIIID 112, 113, 114, 119
Stalingrad 76–7
Stammlager 67
Steinau 109
Steiner 125
Stephenson, Dr Eric 105,109, 204, 210
Stephenson, Freda 205
Stettin 67
Stinson 40
Stirling Castle 154
strafing 66, 119
Stratford on Avon 40, 135
Strathallan 35
Strickland, Ron 171
Strickland, Shirley 156, 170

Suez Canal 35, 154
Suhr, Bill 186
Sulphaguanidine 102
sulphanilamide 101
Sunderland 49
Surfers Paradise 187
Surfers Paradise RSL 209
Sweanor, George 115
switchbacks 15

Tampa crisis 205
Tasmanian Hydroelectric Commission 167
Taylor, Stephen 220
Terry family 197
The Firm 123, 125, 204
The Goons' Show 170
The Great Escape, 25th 184
The Wind and the Rain 109
Tiger Moth 39, 43
Tobolski, Carrie 220
Tom, Dick and Harry 91
Tonder, Ivo 88
Trafalgar Square 37, 44, 45
Twee 104
Twenty Two Temporary Gentlemen 39

University of Melbourne 161
University of Queensland 1
University of Western Australia 23
unter mensch 73, 114
Upper Heyford 49, 51
USAAF 112, 120, 140, 212

V2 94
Vanderstock, Bob 48
VFR 44, 54
Vincent, Group Captain 51
Von Lindeiner, Kommandant 75, 85, 87, 90

Wardell, Rusty 112
Walenn, Tim 220
Walker, 'Black Jack' 31
Walker, Amy 190
Walker, Gus 49, 50
Walker, Sue 10, 165, 167, 170, 174, 178, 180, 181, 182, 183, 184, 187, 225
Walsgrave 42
Warrugul Hospital 171
Weary *see* Dunlop, Sir Edward 'Weary'
Wenthe, George 119, 122
West Australian 30, 64, 98
West Gippsland Hospital, Warragul 172
West Leederville 2, 4, 7, 15, 32, 155, 198
West Leederville Primary School 2, 3, 13, 21
Weston, George 54
Wenthe, George 122
Westray, Jim 40
Wetzlar. 112
White Thursday 62
Whitecross, Jimmy 54
Whiting, Tom 'Piglet' 70
Widdington 40
Williams, Gwenith 4,5, 13, 16, 17, 24, 25, 180
Windsor Hotel 76
Wings 44
Wright, Dr Cliff 189
Wurzburg 118

YMCA 11, 25, 26, 32, 144
You Can't Take It With You 109

Zagan see Sagan
Zipper Club, ACA 203

FORM 414

ROYAL AIR FORCE

PILOT'S FLYING LOG BOOK

Name G. J. CORNISH

PILOT'S LOG BOOK: G J CORNISH

YEAR 1941 MONTH	DATE	AIRCRAFT Type	AIRCRAFT No.	PILOT, OR 1ST PILOT	2ND PILOT, PUPIL OR PASSENGER	DUTY (INCLUDING RESULTS AND REMARKS)
—	—	—	—	—	—	— TOTALS BROUGHT FORWARD
April	1	Hampden	789	Self	Sgt Ratcliffe	Formation
"	2	"	"	"	"	"
"	4	"	"	"	"	To St. Eval
"	5	"	"	"	"	Operations (Brest)
"	6	"	"	"	"	St. Eval to Base
"	7	"	"	"	Sgt Royal	N.F.T.
"	"	"	"	"	Sgt Ratcliffe	Operations (Kiel)
	9	"	"	"	CABW	TEST
	10	"	"	"	SGT RATCLIFFE SGT ROYAL LAC EVANS	NFT
		"	"	"	SGT RATCLIFFE SGT ROYAL LAC EVANS	OPS. DUSSELDORF MISSING

Summary for March 1941
Unit 50 SQN
Date 11/4/41
Signature

1.
2. HAMPDEN
3.
4.

O.C. "A" FLIGHT, No. 50 SQUADRON, S/Ldr

O.C. No. 50 SQUADRON, W/Cdr

GRAND TOTAL [Cols. (1) to (10)] 442 Hrs. 25 Mins.

TOTALS CARRIED FORWARD

THE LAST PAGE:
APRIL 10: MISSSING

GEOFF'S ORIGINAL SILK MAP

HAMPDEN B52

- British Medium Bomber First Flight 21 June 1936
- Entered Service September 1938
- Crew 4
- No power turrets, all guns operated manually.
- The thin cross-section made it almost impossible to change crew positions.
- It was capable of catching and destroying the superior Messerscmitt Bf 110.
- Two 1.000 hp Bristol Pegasus XVII radial Piston engines 409 km/h at 4.205 m; Cruise 269 km/h
- Range 3034 km with 2000 lb of bombs
- Wingspan 21.08 m Wing Area 62.06 m^2
- Length 16.33 m Height 21.08 m Empty Weight 5343 kg Maximum Take Off Weight 8508 kg
- Guns Two forward firing .303 in machine guns with twin .303 in machine guns in dorsal and ventral positions.
- Bombs 4000 lb bomb loads H.P.52 Hampden prototype H.P. 53 Hereford prototype Mk I

BIBLIOGRAPHY

Brickhill, Paul. *The Great Escape*, London Arrow, 1979.

Carroll, Tim. *The great escapers: the full story of the Second World War's most remarkable mass escape*, Edinburgh, Mainstream, 2004.

Durand, Arthur A. *Stalag Luft III: the secret story*, Baton Rouge: Louisiana State University Press, c1988.

Ebury, Sue. *Weary: the life of Sir Edward Dunlop*, Ringwood, Vic., Viking, 1994.

Gill, Anton. *The great escape: the full dramatic story*, London: Headline, 2002.

Natkeil, Richard. *Atlas of World War II*, London, Bison Books, 1985

Newton, Dennis. *First impact*, Maryborough, Qld.: Banner Books, 1997.

Vance, Jonathon F. A. *Gallant Company: the men of the great escape*, California, Pacifica Military History 2000.

Geoff at eight months.

Proud Fred Cornish.

Dot, Geoff, Fred Cornish.

Geoff, three years old.

Perth Boys School, 1935.

Fred's school medals.

Dot and Fred's 50th anniversary.

Geoff, Christmas 1939, Cranwell.

'Wings' award.

50 Squadron, Lindholme.

Hampden B52

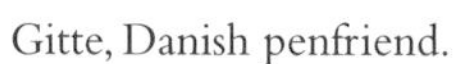

Gitte, Danish penfriend.

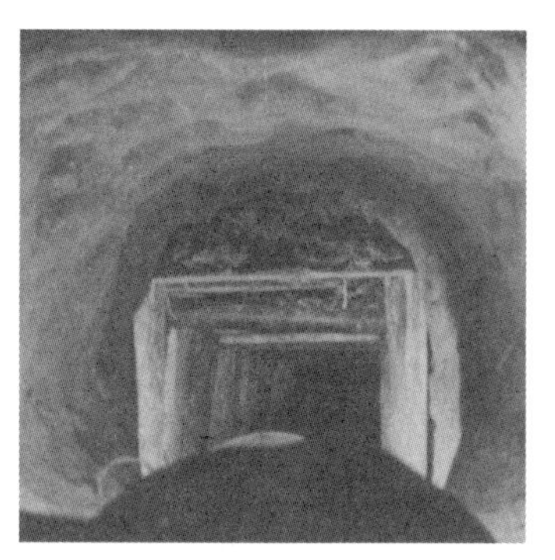

Tunnel.

Inside Geoff's hut.

Aussies at Barth.

POWs, Stalag Luft III.

Waiting to wed.

Myra and Geoff, Perth 1946.

Just married.

Alison and Geoff's wedding.

Geoff at home, 2004.

Geoff and Alison, mid 1980s.

Geoff, Stalag Luft III, 24 March 2004.

Poland, 2004.

Wilhelmina and Geoff, 2004.